Travels in Imperial China

TRAVELS
IN
IMPERIAL CHINA

The explorations and discoveries
of Père David

GEORGE BISHOP

CASSELL

SINKIANG

MONGOLIA

GOBI

PÈRE DAVID'S
JOURNEYS OF
EXPLORATION.

—·—· First Journey
Inner Mongolia
12 March ~ 26 Oct 1866
······ Second Journey
Central China and
Eastern Tibet
May 1868 ~ July 1870
——— Third Journey
Central China
August 1872 ~ April 1874

KANSU

TSINGHAI

Lake Koko Nor

TIBET

Yellow River

R. Yangtze

Himalayas

NEPAL

Lhasa

Muping

Chengtu

SZECHWAN

ASSAM

YUNNAN

BURMA

SIAM

LAOS

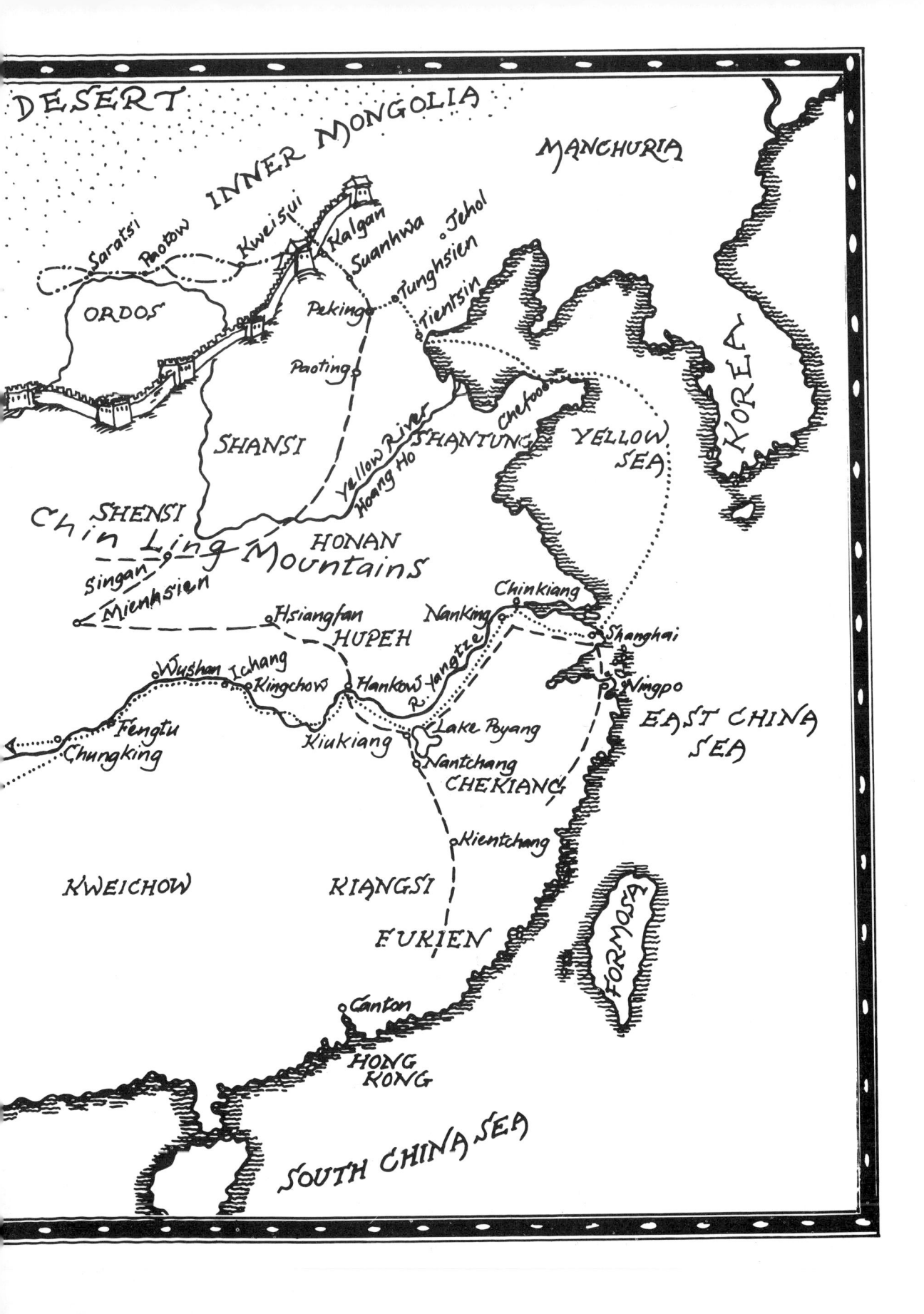

Cassell
Wellington House, 125 Strand
London WC2R 0BB

First published 1990
First paperback edition 1996

Distributed in the United States
by Sterling Publishing Co., Inc.
387 Park Avenue South,
New York, NY 10016-8810

Distributed in Australia
by Capricorn Link (Australia) Pty Ltd
2/13 Carrington Road
Castle Hill, NSW 2154

British Library Cataloguing in Publication Data
Bishop, George
Travels in Imperial China: the explorations and
discoveries of Pere David.
1. China. Description & travel. David, Armand, b.
1826
I. Title II. David, Armand, b. 1826
915.1'043'0924

ISBN 0-304-34802-3

Designed by Vaughan Allen

Typeset by Best-set Typesetter Limited
Printed and bound in Great Britain by Courier International

Cover: *The Great Wall of China* by William Simpson,
courtesy of Phillips/The Bridgeman Art Library

CONTENTS

Père Armand David.

PREFACE

As far as zoos go, I never grow up. I happened to be in Chester, convalescing from a stroke suffered in the South Pacific. How better to spend a day than at Chester Zoo? I was attracted by some deer, a type I had never seen before – Père David's deer. Who on earth is Père David? I wondered. I did not know, nor did anyone else, it seemed. I did eventually find out. More surprisingly, he had also discovered the giant panda. One man and two such discoveries. I was in for an even bigger surprise. Apart from the deer named after him, and the giant panda, David had made innumerable other discoveries, not only of animals but also of plants, such as *Buddleia davidii* and *Clematis armandii*.

I read Helen Fox's translation of Père David's diary. It is an amazing life, fraught with danger. He easily outlived the nine lives of any cat. Yet few people have ever heard of David, even in connection with the much-loved panda.

The modern explorer is weighed down by cameras and linked to the outside world by radio, with stand-by rescue parties not too far away, but David had no supports of this kind. His one luxury – better described as necessity – was his gun, without which he would never have survived to tell his remarkable story. Since David's journals contain no photographs I have included many photographs taken by travellers in China at the same time. The colour prints are David's and the prints of animals were drawn by Alfonse Milne-Edwardes, of the Natural History Museum in Paris, after specimens and descriptions sent to the Museum by David. The colour plates of birds are from *Les Oiseaux de la Chine* by David and Oustalet, of the Paris Museum.

One fault with David , if fault it be, was that he was too modest. On several occasions he was in grave peril of his life, and only extreme coolness and courage saved him. He never dwells on such incidents, and the reader is left to surmise what must have happened. One example of this is an incident when he was surrounded and heavily outnumbered by the dreaded and well-armed *Ch'i-ma-tsei* bandits, who were renowned for their lack of pity. A lone white man in wild, desolate country, with four mules carrying his tempting possessions, was easy prey: they would slit his throat, and leave the rest to the vultures. David's description of the incident is characteristically brief:

> Two years ago I was accosted by eight brigands on horse-back, some of them armed with European weapons. But these rogues soon saw I was not disposed to let myself be despoiled gratuitously; and still less to let myself be killed by such common cut-throats: they would first have to engage in a combat in which some of them might well be hurt. So the *Ch'i-ma-tsei* thought it prudent to retreat.

David must have used his gun to escape with his life. This book is based on David's journals of his travels in China, Mongolia and the borders of Tibet, and his correspondence with the Natural History Museum in Paris. Miss Fox's translation of the Diary has been of great assistance. Where David modestly omits details that reflect to his credit, these have been filled in as they probably occurred. Numerous books of the period have been consulted to ensure that the details represent facts. Having been brought up myself in the heart of Buddhism, on the slopes of the mighty Himalayas, some of the omitted details could be supplied from first-hand knowledge.

George Bishop.

1

THE HOME-COMING

The keen, deep-set eyes under the high forehead peered expectantly out of the carriage. The familiar drizzle did not dampen his delight at being home again. As he stepped down, David filled his lungs to bursting with his native Basque air. The wind played gently with the tufts of white hair that framed the weather-worn, but still handsome, face. Behind him the Nive meandered on its journey down the Basses-Pyrénées to the Bay of Biscay. He looked across to the mountains he loved. As a boy he would often walk ten to twelve hours a day, revelling in the treasures with which Nature rewarded his untiring curiosity. While his friends busied themselves with play, the young David would rather roam the countryside, chasing butterflies, collecting wild flowers, digging up insects, searching for interesting rocks and stones.

Those long arduous walks had served him well in later years when he often had to walk thirty miles a day. Coming from that hardy race that inhabits the south-west of France and the north-east of Spain, he was able to withstand the hardships and privations of his long journeys in China and Mongolia. Then he would often march with nothing to eat or drink all day because in China it was the custom not to eat a midday meal while travelling, and he adhered to local customs and traditions as much as he could. Not that there would be much to eat at the end of the day's journey. His staple meal had been *tsamba*, a flour made of pre-cooked beans and barley, which not only looks like red dust but also tastes like it. But it was the only food for travellers in the desert, since a small bag of it could suffice for a long time. To eat it, one took a handful of the flour, moistened it with water and then rolled it into balls which were swallowed with more than a little courage. Certainly it was a highly nutritious food without which those long journeys could never have been endured. Often, too, it had been so cold that the *tsamba* froze into balls of ice which one ate at the risk of breaking one's teeth. And there were no dentists in those inhospitable regions. Often David did not even have the *tsamba* to eat: he just starved.

11

The traveller, of medium height, picked up his valise, flipped the cape over his shoulder, and set off at a quick pace. Though nearly seventy years old his step was still firm and his gait brisk. He smiled as he greeted passing villagers. Occasionally, he would stop for a chat. At the cemetery gates he turned in. Here lay his father – Fructueux Dominique, doctor, justice of the peace, and mayor of the town of Espelette. Adjoining this grave lay his mother, Rosalie Halsouet, of Bayonne. He noted the somewhat faded flowers before each tombstone.

It was to his father that Armand David owed his great love of the outdoors and of nature. His father had been a keen student of nature and had guided him in his first studies in natural history. It was also from his father, the town doctor, that David had acquired much useful knowledge of hygiene and medicine: knowledge that was to save, not only his own, but other lives when confronted by the ravages of plague, typhus, smallpox, leprosy, rabies, cholera, dysentry and malaria.

There were no antibiotics or 'wonder drugs' in David's day. Nor had the practice of vaccination reached the desolate regions where he travelled. In China and Tibet smallpox was often rife, spread by the great caravans which fanned out from Peking. The disease was understandably held in dread. In Tibet the name would not even be mentioned without the speaker going into a stupor. To contain the epidemics the wretched victims afflicted with smallpox were chased out of their homes and consigned to the summits of mountains or the depths of valleys, where they would soon perish of hunger and privation or become the prey of wild beasts. Leprosy was another common scourge. So, too, was rabies, passed on by the large multitudes of gaunt, famished dogs that prowled everywhere. The situation was not relieved by eliminating the rabid animals: the Tibetans had a profound respect for dogs as they formed one of the ways of disposing of the dead. Rather than cremation, immersion in rivers or lakes, or exposure on the summits of mountains, the most complimentary method of disposing of a corpse was to cut it into pieces which were then fed to the dogs.

In Tartary and Tibet, medicine was practised exclusively by the lamas (monks) but their practices hardly inspired confidence. Their medicines consisted entirely of vegetables pulverised and either infused in water or made up into pills. If the lama physician had no medicine with him, he was by no means disconcerted: he would write the name of the remedy on a piece of paper, moisten the paper with his saliva, then roll it into a pill which the hapless patient would toss down his throat with serene confidence in its efficacy. To swallow the name of the remedy, said the Tartars, amounted to precisely the same thing.

On the occasions when David had run out of what medicines he had managed to carry with him, he was reduced to eating bamboo roots and goosefoot grass as a last-resort remedy. Sometimes these cured him; sometimes they made him worse. At least bamboo and grass had been less hazardous to come by than the fat of a leopard: this was the remedy suggested by a Chinese physician who had diagnosed as bone typhus an illness that had laid David critically ill for several months. Typhus fever is a disease caused by lice, fleas or ticks. If untreated it leads to delirium and coma and finally death.

Further up the mountain were the more recent graves. Here lay his brother, Joseph; there another brother, Louis. There was the grave of his sister, Leone. Of his family he was the only one who had ventured far away from Espelette. How strange, he thought, that here was he, who had undergone every sort of peril one could imagine – attacks by murderous thugs and bandits, the attentions of wolves and leopards and other wild animals, poisoning, stoning, and shipwreck – standing and praying for his family, none of whom had ventured more than a few miles from here. Typhus, malaria, dysentery, sunstroke and other illnesses had struck him down. In the course of eight years he had had no less than five severe (commonly fatal) illnesses and several minor ones. All these he had survived, though often it had meant months of being confined to his coarse goatskin rug which substituted for a bed, in considerable pain and wracked with fever. On three occasions poison had been deliberately placed in his tea. His strong Basque constitution had proved indomitable. He had come out alive from the raging whirlpools and rapids of the Yangtze River. He had kept his feet on the icy, precipitous slopes of the mighty Himalayas.

His was a typical close-knit, devout Basque family. It was this closeness that had buoyed up the young David on his long sojourns in the Celestial Empire of China. Loneliness and homesickness had been the greatest privation he had had to bear as a missionary. Separation from his family for ten or more years, possibly never to see them again, he had come to accept as part of his calling. Letters, at least, had kept the family bonds alive. In his diary he recorded the thrill of receiving news from home:

> 'What a joy and consolation it is to receive letters from relatives, friends and colleagues. The letters are read and reread. We feel that our hearts are in union; we feel alive and for the moment forget where we are; courage returns to us to continue the life of sacrifice.'

But the post between Europe and China took at least six months, if not longer. Often it took over two months for a letter from the interior just to reach

Peking. On some of his explorations, David was away from his base for over two years.

'Armand! Armand!' The shouting jolted David out of his reverie. He turned as he heard his name being called out excitedly. Two young children bore down on him. They helped him with his bag as they chattered non-stop, spilling out all their news.

They entered the comfortable, middle-class dwelling that he had known so well as a boy. His own generation of brothers and sisters had died, but their children and grandchildren always had a great welcome for him whenever he made one of his infrequent visits.

'You've hurt your hand?' the boy inquired.

'No. Why do you ask?'

'Then why do you keep your hand in your pocket?'

An impish smile spread across the explorer's face. Slowly Armand withdrew his hand. The young girl shrieked as he opened his hand. There, on his palm, lay a large black spider. The two youngsters stepped back as he put it down on the floor. The spider wandered curiously round the room. Occasionally, Armand would call it and the spider would run to him.

Chinese symbol for giant panda.

Inevitably the conversation turned to the giant panda. No, he hadn't found any more pandas! It was many years since he had been in China, and had first discovered the rare animal in the forests of Szechwan.

For over five hundred thousand years this lovable animal had lived hidden from the rest of the world by a dense, impenetrable 'bamboo curtain'. At one time it had ranged quite widely throughout China and into Burma. But as the climate had become drier and as human poachers had begun to encroach on its habitat, the giant panda had been forced to retreat to its last stronghold, the remote, inaccessible wilderness, between 5,000 and 11,000 feet (1,500 and 3,300 m) in altitude, in the mountain regions of Eastern Tibet and the provinces of Szechwan, Yunnan and Shensi in China. Even in those regions, the animal is extremely rare and its numbers are being reduced year by year, not only because of the activities of unscrupulous hunters and poachers but because of the peculiar diet on which the pandas live. They feed on what is known in China as 'arrow' bamboo and sometimes this crop fails; the fact that bamboos flower and produce seeds only once in their lifetime makes the situation even more precarious.

Giant panda.

The children were curious about the panda's black markings – the little black nose, the pirate's black patches over each eye, the little round black ears, the black-stockinged legs. The smiling David told them the Chinese legend about the strange animal.

A long time ago, high in the mountains of central China a young girl grew up with a family of giant pandas. At that time they all wore snow-white fur coats. One day a mountain leopard – one of the many in those wild parts – attacked a baby panda. The girl went to the rescue of the baby panda, but in saving the panda's life she lost her own. The giant pandas were all very, very sad. At the funeral all the pandas wore black on their shoulders, arms and legs as a sign of mourning. As they cried they wiped their eyes with their paws, thus making the black eye-patches. In their sadness they put their heads in their paws, thus giving themselves their black noses. And when the pandas reached up they touched their ears, which also turned black. And the giant pandas remember the little girl's bravery, by wearing those black markings even today.

The two children had listened spellbound. They wanted to hear more: how did he find the first one? The famous explorer smiled: that was a long story. It is, in part, the narrative of this book.

卐卐卐卐卐卐卐卐卐

It was now some weeks since David's pet spider had crawled to and fro at his command around the sitting-room of the family home at Espelette. Today it sat immobile on his desk in his room on the second floor of the House of his Order, the Vincentians, or Congregation of the Missions, founded in Paris in 1625 by Saint Vincent de Paul. Their house was in the Rue de Sèvres in Saint-Lazarre: hence their name of Lazarists. The French Revolution had wreaked havoc on the Order, but it had picked up again. His House had been David's home since he had returned from his third and last exploration in China in 1874.

The spider stirred as the door handle turned. It settled back into its motionless pose as Brother Masingue sank into the tatty chair that stood by the window. It had been a hectic time for the brother. All day messages had been pouring into the House; there was a constant stream of callers. For him the time had been particularly sad. Yesterday he had helped carry the body of David to lie before the main altar in the chapel. He had shared in the vigil which his fellow brothers, swollen in numbers by the young seminarians and students who had been David's pupils, had kept throughout the night. He had been sent here to help sort and clear out David's room.

The room gave the impression of total bedlam. There were books and papers everywhere, even on the floor. On the walls were drawings and prints of all kinds of plants and animals. In a corner stood a pile of trays containing butterflies of dazzling hues, their wings all carefully spread out and pinned. There were cabinets containing beetles of different sizes and shapes and colours. Here was a stuffed owl; there more stuffed birds. Where was he to begin?

Brother Masingue sat down again in the rather worn chair near the window. Slowly it became apparent that there was some order in the seeming chaos. The papers seemed to be in piles. He went over to the bookshelves holding both new and musty volumes. He opened one of the tomes. The cover read '*Les Oiseaux de la Chine*, A. David & M. E. Oustalet, Paris 1877'. Here were page after page of magnificent colour drawings of the birds David had discovered on his travels in China. He carefully put the heavy tome back in its place on the shelf and ran his fingers along the books. He picked out a small fat book: '*Journal de mon troisième voyage d'exploration dans l'Empire Chinois.* Paris, Libraire Hachette et Cie, 79 Boulevard St. Germain, 1875'. He flipped over the pages. Here was a map of the three long journeys David had undertaken. He placed his finger at the dots and dashes that indicated the first journeys of 1864 and 1866: his finger moved from Peking along to the Great Wall of China, to the great Yellow River, the Hoang, in Inner Mongolia, running between the Ordos Mountains and the forbidding Gobi Desert. He took his finger off the page to gather the full picture. To the right lay Manchuria, to the north Mongolia, to the west Sinkiang and Tibet. His eyes caught the names Szechwan, Chengtu, Muping.

The map intrigued him. His finger began to trace out the route of David's second journey, made between May 1868 and July 1870. Over two years away from his colleagues in wild inhospitable territory. Peking to Tientsin to Chefoo, across the Yellow Sea to Shanghai. His finger traced the course of the mighty Yangtze River from Nanking, Kiukiang, Hankow, the rapids of Ichang, Wushan, Chungking, Muping (now Paoking in Sikang). Muping was where David had discovered the giant panda. He fingered through the book for illustrations. Perhaps there was one of the famous animal. But there were no illustrations at all, just narrative. He glanced at the route of David's last journey, nearly two years again, from August 1872 to April 1874, then placed the chunky little volume back in its place.

Large tomes took over a whole shelf to themselves. He moved nearer: they were volumes marked '*Nouvelles Archives du Muséum d'histoire*

Naturelle de Paris'. He picked out one at random. It was Tome 6: 'M. A. Franchet, *Plantae Davidianae ex Sinarum Imperio'*.

He moved across to some other shelves, and inclined his head to read some of the titles more easily. 'C. Oberthuer, *Études d'Entomologie*, 1876'. He took down a large volume and opened it: '*Recherches pour servir a l'Histoire Naturelle des Mammifères*, Libraire de L'Académie de Médicine, Paris 1868–1874'.

He moved over to the large desk, where the black spider kept its impassive vigil. There were letters from all parts of Europe, and others from his beloved China, from Constantinople, from Tunisia, from Java.

He began a cursory glance at the contents of the drawers in the desk. Here was an envelope addressed simply 'Monsieur Armand, Paris'. With no street number or house number it had reached its destination. Another drawer contained some parchment scrolls. He opened one: it was headed 'Académie des Sciences, Paris', and was admitting the recipient to membership of that august body. It was dated 1872. He carefully rolled up the scroll and put it back. Here was another scroll: it was recording the award of a gold medal at the Sorbonne jointly by the Société Géographique, the Réunion de Savants and the Société de France. He flipped through some other pieces of parchment. Here was the one he wanted to see. It was from the French government dated 1896, awarding the recipient the Cross of the Legion of Honour. The sash lay carefully folded in the drawer. It had obviously never been worn. Brother Masingue stroked his hand over the smooth, red moiré before closing the drawer.

As the organ pealed the bars of the Requiem the church echoed to the choir's '*In paradisum deducant te Angeli* ... May the Angels lead you into paradise. May the Martyrs await your coming and bring you into the Holy City, the heavenly Jerusalem. May a choir of Angels welcome you, and with the poor man Lazarus of old, may you enjoy eternal rest.'

They laid to rest the man of many lives in one corner of the Lazarist cemetery. The graves were all indistinguishable: green mounds each surmounted by a plain wooden cross, bearing only name, year of birth and of death, and at the foot of each cross a posy of flowers. Except one grave: an admirer had placed a toy panda there, to keep its lone vigil over one who had done so much in his lifetime for the welfare and preservation of animals of every variety and for the conservation of the habitats in which they lived.

2

BAPTISM BY DUEL

A cloud of pigeons with striped tails winged away towards the hills. Jujubes, apricots and stunted elms lined the road. Sitting astride a mule hour after hour, six hours in the morning and six hours after noon, was a tedious affair.

A sudden thud jolted David out of his reverie. His mule snorted disapproval as it was pulled to a sudden halt. The jingling of the little bells adorning the mule's neck, as in his native Basque country, subsided. David turned round. There was Thomè, prostrate, face-down in the coarse ground; his mule stood by, an air of astonished disbelief on its face. Ouang Thomè was a Chinese helper accompanying David on his way to Jehol (now Chengteh), 125 miles (200 km) north east of the capital Peking, and near the Mongolian and Manchurian borders. If David was to acquire the Chinese language, learn their habits and customs, and something of the natural history of the vast country, he could only do this with travelling. The Empire had only been open to Europeans in the last twenty years: there was a great deal to find out and explore. Since arriving in China in 1862 David had collected numerous interesting species of plants and animals in the Peking plains and in the western and northern hills surrounding the capital. This had only whetted his curiosity more.

David burst out laughing as Thomè picked himself up and dusted the ochre sand off his tunic and face. The steady metronomic rhythm of his mule's gait had lulled him to sleep. Thomè was not amused.

Besides the two mules carrying David and Thomè, there were two other mules carrying the luggage. In addition to bedding and clothing, David carried all the gear necessary for hunting and for collecting specimens of plants and animals – arsenic, salt and alum required for taxidermy and for herbarium specimens, cabinets of all sizes, empty bottles, and more. Added to this was his Mass kit, for he was first and foremost a priest.

From the suburb of Pei-t'ang located in the Tartar sector of Peking, where

The great imperial stone road leading
out of Peking.

his College was located, David had left the teeming city through the north
gate. At first the road had been wide, but soon it was nothing but grooves and
ruts worn parallel to each other. The carriage portion of the road was just a
quagmire of mud and putrid filth, deep enough to stifle and bury the smaller
beasts of burden, like donkeys and mules, that frequently fell into it. While
these carcasses added to the general stench, the innumerable thieves lurking
nearby soon disposed of the loads. Carriage wheels that fell into the deep holes
made by missing paving stones broke not only axles but also the bones of the
passengers. The footpath was a narrow, rugged, slippery line on either side of
the road, just wide enough for one person. Incessant arguments as to right of
way, punctuated with filthy abuse, and sometimes even fisticuffs, were common. The avenue leading to the tombs of the Imperial Ming dynasty was lined
with huge marble statues of elephants, camels, horses and other animals. In
front of small hills covered in pines, junipers and large-leaved oaks, were
magnificent monuments and pagodas. The Emperor's palace with its many

incongruous fairy-like buildings appeared almost unreal before us.

Slowly the plains gave way to the granite hills of the north. David, Thomè and the mules made their way across the wild landscape, laboriously covering the distance as a caterpillar eats away a leaf. No one spoke, for in China silence was the rule while travelling, and in China everybody obeyed the traditional customs. The going became tedious with only the occasional flock of wild geese or grey herons, flying north in an inverted V formation, helping to break the monotony. Presently their peace was shattered. They could see ahead of them an angry, swirling wave of brown dust and sand bearing down on them. David hastily made sure his gun was securely wrapped to protect its breeches from the approaching sand. Suddenly it was like riding on a sea of sand as the brown rivulets rushed past the feet of their animals. Their faces smarted as the angry wind shot tiny particles of earth at them. David could no longer retain his cramped position on the mule; he couldn't even see its head. The riders were forced to dismount and cover their faces to avoid being blinded. In seconds everything was deeply coated with fine dust: their clothes, their baggage, their eyes, their mouths, their noses, their ears. The sand stuck to their sweating limbs. They could scarcely pry apart their eyelids. The black and grey mules had metamorphosed into brown as if by magic.

When the dust-storm abated David was pleased to see in the distance the flag which heralded an inn. They had covered over 30 miles (48 km) that day. Law stipulated that inns be placed at distances of 30–35 miles (48–56 km). Thus, by choice or by force, one was obliged to travel these long distances each day if one hoped to find shelter for the night. When he eventually appeared, the conical cap on the innkeeper's head, with his queue or pigtail folded into it, confirmed he was a Muhammadan. David was glad. In China there were two kinds of inn: inns where they fought against brigands and inns where they did not. In general, Muslims were more ready to take up arms than the more placid Chinese. Of course, prices at the former were four times or more expensive than at the latter.

The next day they set off at daybreak, having swallowed some tea without sugar. A group of rock partridges continued to feed and cackle on the side of the road, not bothering to move out of the way. They were obviously not used to being disturbed by passers-by. David noted the various types of birds he encountered: flocks of geese and herons, magpies, rooks, jackdaws, the occasional woodpecker. The flora was disappointing, however,: no primulas or jonquils to herald spring, as in Europe. In a gully he noted the daphne, with its yellow flowers, growing amid the stones, and he noted the bruised yellow fronds of some rare ferns new to him.

Meeting traffic in a narrow defile invariably led to arguments – and often worse.

Suddenly, calamity! This was one of those confrontations David was dreading. A wild man, his face contorted with rage, confronted David. With his left hand he held on to the rein of his camel, with the other he gesticulated wildly. Astride his tiny mule David appeared a midget as the camel with its irate rider towered over him. Even the Bactrian, its barbaric wool-crested head held aloft, looked down contemptuously. The loud chorus of abuse coming from the other camel drivers who had appeared behind the leader drowned the jingling of bells around their animals' necks.

David spoke well above the volume of his normal voice. He had to, to be heard. He explained that he had right of way through the narrow defile. The camel party should have waited for him since he had entered the narrow gorge before they had.

The camel party, however, had obviously decided not to wait for a few puny mules. They would bully their way if necessary. His calm reasoning was jeered down. But David held his ground: to give way was to lessen your dignity as a traveller.

'Ride him down,' a voice yelled out from behind the man confronting David. The camel stood there, dignified, motionless, like some ancient sphinx from its far-off country of origin.

David realised this impasse could not go on forever. He began to feel increasing alarm, despite his outward show of bravado. How could the impasse be broken without too much loss of face on either side?

The wild man shouted out something and then, in a flash, drew a fiendish-looking cutlass from the pack saddle fitted round the Bactrian's double hump. David's mule instinctively moved back. David steadied the frightened mule and, equally swiftly, drew his gun from his saddle. He cocked the rifle and pointed it at the man snarling savagely at him.

The situation was now desperate: David and Thomè were heavily outnumbered. The defile was so narrow that only one animal could pass at a time. But they had one advantage. David, on his mule, was armed with a weapon he could use at a distance against the wild man on the camel, still flourishing his sword menacingly. But what David wanted least of all was to have to use his gun. The haughty camel, still wearing its coat of wool, suddenly surrendered its dignity as it swooped down to bite David's mule on the neck.

A flock of grey and black jackdaws, migrating to the north, swept over the defile. A vulture swooped low, perhaps suspecting easy pickings.

The wild man guessed that the *Kang-jen* (Westerner) came from Peking. His pride gave way to his native sense of business. All goods coming from Peking were highly prized, and merchants took care to ensure their goods were labelled to show their Peking origin.

Did David have any goods for bartering – like snuff or tea, or tobacco or dried fruits or, especially, *sam-shoo*, the Chinese whisky? David parted with some tea and tobacco: the mules advanced.

One of the renowned *Ch'i-ma-tsei* (mounted bandits)
who even ate the hearts of their victims.

They began climbing the foothills leading to Jehol. A large, partly ruined pagoda looked down benevolently on them. David would have liked to talk to the *bonze*, or Buddhist monk, who allegedly lived his entire life, winter and summer, on the mountain. But it was late. And the country was safe at night only for the geese heading north and for the field larks and the owls.

Swirling dust clouds warned of another impending sandstorm. They halted. As the clouds grew nearer their anxiety mounted: the whirlpools of dust were accompanied by a strange roar. Neither David nor Thomè had experienced anything like this before. They waited as the sand and the sound grew closer. 'My God!' thought David, 'it must be a whole troop of cavalry.'

Out of the dusty gloom a wild and uncouth figure appeared on horseback in front of them, like some weird apparition. Seven other horsemen pulled their steeds to a trot to join their leader. They shouted instructions to one another. David realised he was hopelessly outnumbered and his mules were no match for the speed of the horses. There was no escape. These were the renowned *Ch'i-ma-tsei*, mounted bandits, who even ate the hearts of their unfortunate victims. One of the horsemen moved round, obviously intending to encircle him. Only swift action could save them. David fired at the horse's feet, and it leapt into the air, hurling its surprised rider to the ground. A shot at the foot of the horse of another cut-throat who was about to come behind him on the other side stopped horse and rider in their tracks. Bullets spoke the only language they knew. David levelled his gun at the leader. No one moved; only a quail became airborne, rudely disturbed by the noise. David kept the leader in his sights; the man glowered back. David had the advantage: the leader, in his confident arrogance, had not drawn his gun. The weapon was attached to a wooden saddle, held on the horse's back by two narrow leather girdles, one round the animal's belly, the other close behind its forelegs. The men waited for a signal from their leader, who sat statuesque on his horse. Only a torrent of urine from one of the horses broke the vast silence. The sweat poured off David's face, the beads of perspiration beginning to trickle into his eyes, obscuring his vision.

After what seemed an eternity the leader slowly let go of his rope bridle and lifted up his arms, wondering if David would fire. When his arm was vertical he called out something which was incomprehensible to David, and slowly turned his horse away. After some hesitation the others slowly turned their horses and followed their leader.

The experience had been more than unnerving. As for Thomè, he had been on the point of beginning the peculiar low wilting wail which the Chinese incant when they know death is inescapable and imminent.

The mule caravan continued its journey, with only the jingling of bells round the mules' necks intruding on the vast silence. They reached the place where they had been told an inn existed, but there was no sign of it. A cloud of smoke told of a recent fire. David and Thomè could scarcely believe their eyes. What had obviously once been an inn had been razed to the ground. Huddled in a group were those who had survived the vicious attack. All their possessions had been pillaged; some still bled from the sabre blows they had received when they tried to put out the fire with buckets of water. From the description given by the poor wretches it was clear that it was the bandits so recently encountered by David who had been responsible. David gave what medical help he could. He and Thomè then shared their meagre *tsamba* meal with the victims. They got what little sleep they could, their backs pressed against the bodies of their mules.

The terrain was becoming more mountainous. Winter was giving way to spring, and the ice was beginning to melt and break here and there, although enough remained to cause the mules to slip. The ascent of one of the many passes was becoming increasingly difficult. The mules skidded wildly as their hoofs flayed the layer of sand and rubble from the black ice beneath. In parts the track was almost impassable; the mules needed the agility of ibexes to negotiate the slippery boulders. David dismounted: holding on to his mule's

The going up many of the passes was extremely difficult.
Mules would skid wildly as their hoofs flayed the layer
of sand from the black ice beneath.

tail made the mountain travel less fatiguing both for him and his mule. Moreover, travelling on foot had the advantage of enabling him to observe the flora and fauna at closer quarters.

David was relieved when he finally reached Jehol. He had learnt more about Chinese culture and customs than either he or his superiors had bargained for! It was pleasant to be with colleagues at the mission station; to have something more tasty than *tsamba* to eat; to sleep on a bed instead of on the floor in his goatskin rug in a dirty crowded inn, or out in the open. The Inspector of Darkness banged out the official night alarm on his tom-tom. The noise would frighten off the wolves and tigers that frequented the region, especially the wolves prevalent in the mountains of north China. In a nearby village more than a dozen people had been devoured by wolves in the space of a month. But David heard nothing; he was too exhausted.

The next few months David spent scouring the countryside for plants and animals, birds and insects, anything that would add to the collection he was building up at the College. In due course David's museum acquired such renown as to become the property of the Emperor of China.

Although anything but aggressive by nature, David had learnt that if the occasion arose he was quite able to take care of himself. This gave him confidence in his forays into the desert haunts where the most interesting plants and animals were to be found. Once or twice this confidence turned to carelessness which nearly cost him his life, as when rain and snow caught him unprepared up in the mountains. He had entered the dens of wolves, bears, wild boars, leopards, panthers and even the long-haired royal tiger, native to the forests of Manchuria. It was quite common for hunters and wood-cutters who ventured into the forests to disappear without trace – and he had not even bothered to carry his gun!

On his eventual return to Peking David sent many of his zoological and botanical specimens to the Museum of Natural History in Paris. This action was to change the course of his life.

3

SAVED FROM EXTINCTION

It was September 1865. David seemed to be swimming against a torrent of people and stray dogs. Skullcaps, turbans, hats edged with lambskin, shaven heads: all bobbed up and down in a sea of humanity. He stopped to let a Tartar bowman, resplendent on a magnificent steed, trot past. A bare-footed rice vendor, in short pants and black tunic, a wide-brimmed straw hat protecting him from the sun, steadied the two baskets suspended across his shoulders and came to a halt. He had obviously never seen a white man before. Old amahs in black pants and jackets, ragged urchins in tow, and not-so-old amahs, babies on hips, also stopped to stare. Even an old opium addict, pipe in hand, was roused from his reverie by the strange appearance of the white man. Alone among the throng, a bare-chested peasant in black cotton trousers tied at the ankles above his straw sandals, a long bamboo suspended over one shoulder from one end of which hung a basket of fruit and vegetables, from the other a basket of fowls and ducks, continued jogging, too set in motion to stop. David lashed out at the pick-pocket's hand that had wormed its way into his jacket.

How tame the birds were! A Manchu carried a grosbeak on his left fist, a warbler nestled on his right shoulder. Some minutes later a well-dressed man threw his falcon into the air. David watched it wing away, circle, and then unerringly return to its owner's arm, despite the huge throng of people.

Peking was built within grandiose walls of imposing dimensions, 40 feet (12 m) high and 64 feet (20 m) broad at the top, arranged in two large quadrilaterals. To leave the city, David passed through the first gate, a massive folding portal, then through a long tunnel under the wall to another portal; he crossed over what was once a moat and was then out on the dusty road leading south. The road was full of ruts, making life most uncomfortable for those travelling by cart or wagon; the poorer travelled in wheelbarrows. David hurried so as to outpace the gangs of ragged urchins with swollen bellies who tried to attach themselves to him. He stepped across the road to avoid a fierce

A Peking street.

red-eyed hound, turning round only when he felt he was at a safe distance from the brute. Innumerable lanes ran off the main road; low mud hovels nestling among larger brick buildings. Beggars, unfortunate bearers of all manner of diseases, some of them half-naked, swarmed the lanes or lay about on door-steps. He saw a gaudily painted Confucian temple, ornately carved with dragons and phoenixes; as he passed, the familiar smell of incense being burnt by the tablet-worshippers greeted him. Defiantly confronting the temple was the dome of a mosque, surmounted by a gold crescent. He crossed the road again to let pass a dromedary being led by a string through its nose.

David was heading for the Imperial Hunting Park at Hai-tzu, several miles south of the city. He had heard reports about the *mi-lou*, who were also referred to as *ssu-pu-hsiang* – 'the four characteristics which do not match'. This was the name given by the Chinese to a strange animal which was supposed to have the antlers of a stag, the hooves of a cow, the neck of a camel and the elongated tail of a donkey. No one that David knew had ever seen such a strange animal. He had wondered if it really existed, or whether it was just another legendary animal like the unicorn, dragon or phoenix, which filled the pages of Chinese literature.

A small herd of the animal was supposed to be kept in the Imperial Hunting Park at Hai-tzu. Entry to the Park was forbidden to all Europeans, as, indeed, it was to most of the local populace, on pain of death. High forbidding walls, extending 45 miles (72 km) in circumference, and under constant guard of Tartar soldiers, ensured that the Park kept its secrets. David had determined to find out if the *mi-lou* really existed.

The high walls of the Imperial Park came into view. David skirted the 20-foot (6-m) high wall in the hope of finding an aperture which would give him a sight of the strange animal with 'the four characteristics'. Eventually fortune smiled on the determined Basque: in the distance piles of new bricks and sand indicated that part of the wall was under repair. David quickened his steps. The workmen had obviously finished their labours for the day. He glanced about him, then gingerly climbed on top of the pile of bricks.

It was true. The *mi-lou* existed. There they were, fawn-grey in colour, browsing in the sparse grass. He had never seen any deer like these before. They seemed smaller than the northern elk or reindeer. The females appeared to have no antlers. Their cry resembled more the bray of a donkey than the call of a deer. Their gait, too, was more like that of a mule than of other deer he had seen. But it was their long donkey-like tails which baffled David: it was this feature that distinguished the animal from any other kind of deer or elk he had ever seen.

David made notes of what he was seeing. Little did he realise he was then the first westerner ever to set eyes on the species of deer that was one day to bear his name – *Elaphurus davidianus* – Père David's deer. What David also did not know then was that the herd of curious deer before him was the only herd still living in the world; they were already extinct in their wild state.

David hurried back to the College where he taught science. It was now dark and dangerous for a foreigner to be out at night. He apologised profusely as he bumped into a coolie carrying earthenware jars of rice wine suspended from a bamboo yoke across his back. He apologised again as he nearly knocked over an old man with dropsy, struggling on his crutch. He could not fail to notice the lavishly painted lady borne past in a sedan chair; her face was painted from her neck to her eyelids with white, rose and blue paint; her lips and ears, too, were painted. She reminded him of one of the dolls his sister used to

A bare-foot rice vendor, with a Tartar
bowman in the background.

One of the gates leading out of the capital, Peking.
Note the massive walls with forts on top.

play with as a young child. He re-entered the gateway to the city he had left earlier that day. He swung past what had been the cathedral, built by the Jesuits, but long since disused, the cross surmounting it long since dismantled, and services within its walls forbidden.

David determined he would approach the French Legation to obtain a specimen of the strange deer through diplomatic channels. All his attempts through this route failed, however. He would have to try less conventional methods, and this would be dangerous. The penalty for killing one of these animals was death. It was said that some of the soldiers guarding the *mi-lou* in the Park would occasionally secretly kill one or two of the animals for food. But even they would never risk their lives by daring to sell any part of the animal, not even the prized antlers. From the fourth to the seventh moon the antlers of the stags sent out new shoots which contained a kind of half-coagulated blood called *Lu-jung*. This *Lu-jung* was highly prized in Chinese *materia medica* and would fetch exorbitant prices in solid silver.

Once again David battled his way through the motley maelstrom of people and animals to the Imperial Park at Hai-tzu. He caught his breath as hundreds of pretty little birds fluttered out of captivity into the sky. A rich innkeeper had bought cages of the birds and immediately set them free. David bided his time and when the way was clear scaled up the high wall.

The Tartar guard turned at hearing something, unslinging the rifle from his shoulder. David addressed him politely, at the same time brandishing a string of copper cash. (In China there was no money except copper cash. Silver was in ingots and was regarded as merchandise, its value changing according to weather and place, and was exchanged for cash as and when necessary.) Cautiously the guard stepped forward. David inquired about the *mi-lou*. He brandished the copper cash more obviously.

High forbidding walls, extending to 45 miles (72 km) in circumference and under constant guard of Tartar soldiers, kept the secrets of the Imperial Hunting Park at Hai-tzu.

Could he do business with the guard? David wondered. The guard eyed the cash. A cube of tobacco that fell at his feet brought a smile, followed by an uncomfortable pause. 'Silver or one's neck?' the guard was thinking. Execution by decapitation was particularly dreaded, especially as, in accordance with custom, the body was left to rot in the highway, at the mercy of starving mongrels and swooping carrion.

As from time immemorial, money won. They did a deal. For a sum of 20 taels the guard would obtain for David the hides and bones of a pair of deer.

It was the end of January, 1866. Peking was in the firm grip of winter as David set out to keep his rendezvous with the Park guard. He pulled his fur-lined cap down over his face and his collar up to keep out the biting wind, and also to make himself as anonymous as possible. It was almost like home,

A Tartar soldier with matchlock.

trudging through the soft snow, except that here and there the mantle of white was stained yellow with the urine of passing camels.

The break in the Park wall had been repaired. He pressed closer to the wall to gain more shelter from the icy wind. A throat was cleared on the other side of the wall. David moved nearer to where this sound had come from and began to clear his own throat. A bag thudded into the snow not far from where he was standing. He picked up the bag and began feeling its contents. There were no bones, only hide. The guard had kept half his promise: so, too, would David. From under his jacket David pulled out the cash, divided it into two, and hurled one lot of 10 taels over the wall. It landed with a faint thud on the soft snow the other side. There was a long pause, only the snow whispering. Another much noisier thud broke the silence. David picked up the sack that had landed near him and felt the contents. The guard had kept his promise and provided the bones as well. David swung his arm and the second instalment of 10 taels sailed over the wall. He secreted the two bags under his coat and made off, quickening his pace as he went. He had to reach Peking before the city gates were closed for the night.

Once safely within the city walls he slackened his pace. But not too much: he did not want to be caught red-handed, carrying the remains of a *mi-lou*. A rickshaw coolie, hat in hand, rested. David contemplated doing the same, but thought better of it. A large carved wooden dragon, painted green and gold, over the doorway signalled a pawnshop. The owner was hurriedly putting away his silks and fur coats.

Passing under one of the many triumphal arches David entered the suburb of Tih-sing. Numbers of people with bed-rolls on their heads and carrying bundles of clothing were looking for a sleeping place for the night. Men were drinking rice wine and playing cards in the inns and gambling parlours. An emaciated body sprawled outside an opium den, like a spectre among the dead. A pimp touted for business. A mandarin, his identity masked behind the curtain that covered the sedan chair, haggled over price. A smell of bean curd and spiced noodles mingled with that of sweat, cheap fat and rice wine. He would have liked to warm his hands on the charcoal brazier in which a pavement vendor was frying pieces of battered snake. Rich food smells hung on the frosty air; paper lanterns were shining gold in the dusk.

David was glad to see the gates of the College where he taught. In his room he carefully opened the two sacks, barely able to believe his eys. Here were the skins and bones of an adult female and a young female *mi-lou*, hardly touched. Delighted, he ran his fingers through the long donkey-like tail. He examined the bones and the strange hooves like those of a cow. The large spreading feet indicated that the animal's natural habitat was marshy ground. Carefully, he packed away his treasures.

For the next few evenings, as soon as he had dismissed his last class, David would head straight for the College laboratory. Here he would carefully go through the laborious process of curing the animal parts.

Alphonse Pichon, an attaché at the French Legation, was about to return to Paris. David made for the Legation. Pichon was happy to take his treasure to the Natural History Museum in Paris.

The *mi-lou*, which was also called the *ssu-pu-hsiang*, or 'the four characteristics which do not match', since it was described as having the antlers of a stag, the hooves of a cow, the neck of a camel, and the elongated tail of a donkey. It is known today as Père David's deer (*Elaphurus davidianus*).

A sedan chair.

There was a sequel to this meeting. Several months later David was summoned to the French Embassy in Peking. He wondered if he had incurred the displeasure of the Chinese Government by 'obtaining' the skin and bones of a *mi-lou* and sending it abroad. Would he be expelled, just as he was starting his missionary work in the East?

David was received politely enough by Count de Bellonet. In front of the dapper little diplomat lay a pile of very official-looking documents, all heavily headed with monograms. The Count picked up one of these, from Mr Milne-Edwardes, the Director of the Museum of Natural History in Paris. It was to him that David had consigned the skin and bones of the *mi-lou* via Alphonse Pichon. David's worst fears were realised. The diplomat put down this letter and picked up another, embossed Ministry of External Affairs, Paris. So this was the expulsion order. Count de Bellonet began reading the letter:

> I attach a copy of a letter I have received from Monsieur Henri Milne-Edwards, Director of the Museum of Natural History in Paris. You will observe what the letter has to say about an animal he refers to as *Elaphurus davidianus*.
>
> As a result of several representations from members of the science faculty of the University of Paris and of members of the Académie des Sciences, Monsieur Victor Duruy, Minister of Public Instruction, has asked me to prevail upon your good offices to seek to obtain living specimens of this animal for shipment to the motherland.... Yours fraternally,
> Minister of External Affairs

Again, Count de Bellonet peered over his pince-nez. David was taken aback. Was he hearing right?

The chargé d'affaires called for Monsieur Pichon. He led the two of them behind the building which served as the offices, and into the Embassy gardens.

Count de Bellonet did not speak; Monsieur Pichon mentioned only such trivialities as the weather.

David let out a gasp. Here, in front of him, were three magnificent specimens of *mi-lou*: a male, resplendent with its magnificent antlers, and beside it two young females. David was speechless. The two others were smiling to themselves. Count de Bellonet put his finger to his lips. 'A state secret', Monsieur Pichon explained. The chargé d'affaires had diplomatically persuaded minister Hen-Tchy, an in-

Père David's deer: adult male obtained more diplomatically through the French embassy and sent by David to the Museum of Natural History, Paris.

fluential *kuan* or mandarin and superintendent of the imperial estates, to let the animals accidentally stray out of the Park.

Unfortunately the male *mi-lou* did not survive long in the gardens of the French Embassy. Count de Bellonet gave the body to David who, in due course, sent it to the Museum of Natural History in Paris. Professor Milne-Edwardes now held three specimens of *mi-lou* – an adult male, an adult female and a young female – on which to base his scientific description of Père David's deer, *Elaphurus davidianus*. The colour plate shows the actual female specimens sent by David to Paris and preserved in the Museum.

The European zoos were very interested in this 'new' animal. In 1867 Sir Rutherford Alcock, the British Ambassador in Peking, secured a pair of Père David's deer, but they died before they could be shipped to England. In 1869 Robert Swinhoe, the British Consul, brought a pair of the deer to London Zoo, but the female died in 1870 and the male two years later. In 1870 David sent a live male deer to the Jardin des Plantes in Paris; about the same time a pair was also sent by the French Embassy.

The herd of *mi-lou* in the Imperial Park near Peking contained the only surviving examples of the species in the entire world at that time. In 1894 the flooding of the River Han breached the Park walls, allowing many of the precious herd to escape. These were soon slaughtered by the famine-stricken peasants, and what remained of the herd were killed off by foreign troops encamped in the Park during the Boxer Rebellion of 1900. It was very nearly the end of another species, but fortunately the living specimens sent to Paris in 1870 survived and bred. In 1896 a pair of descendents of these deer were sent to England and formed a herd on the Duke of Bedford's estate at Woburn

Abbey in Bedfordshire. The wheel of fortune turned full circle in 1957 when the Zoological Society of London presented four young Père David's deer to Peking, so that the species which had originally come from China could re-establish itself in its former natural habitat. In November 1985, nineteen more of the rare animals were returned to the Imperial Hunting Park, Peking, by the Marquess of Tavistock, the Duke of Bedford's great-grandson.

A group of *kuans* or mandarins.

4

SAMBDATCHIEMDA

David froze as he watched the shadow of a head and shoulders advance along the volcanic soil towards him. As he looked up he started. The last time he had met the *Ch'i-ma-tsei* bandits he had had the advantage: his gun was cocked and levelled on their leader. All he now held in his blackened hands was the petrified bone of an elephant.

The man was much the same height as David, but considerably broader in the chest – obviously a powerful man. His visage instilled awe and alarm. He was clothed in a huge sheepskin rudely drawn round the waist and tied by a thick camel-hair rope. His hair, black, curly and greasy, hung in long matted locks down his shoulders. His right arm was bare, the sleeve thrown back completely, exposing a huge hand grasping the hilt of a long broad sabre which passed through his girdle just below the chest.

David could not but admire the presence of the man. David himself carefully wrapped up against the cold; there was he with arms and legs and much of his chest bare. To wear warm clothing against the freezing conditions was considered a mark of pusillanimity among these brave warriors. Brave rascals like them feared nothing, neither men nor the elements.

David fully expected him to clap the sabre to his neck and bawl out, 'Your money or your life, venerable brother!' 'Venerable brother' could then divest himself of his mule, his valuables and his clothing. He had heard stories where the armed bandits and brigands who terrorised those parts would strip travellers, not merely of horse and possessions, but even of the clothes they wore, leaving them naked to perish from cold and hunger. The villagers lived in mortal dread of these men. Hardly a house did not carry the mark of their visitations and pillage. If 'venerable brother' decided not to co-operate the sabre would settle matters unilaterally and expeditiously.

The huge brute of a man advanced on David who instinctively drew back. A broad smile spread over the savage man's face. This courteous salutation

Sambdatchiemda, David's guide, who had
accompanied Fathers Huc and Gabet to Lhasa,
capital of Tibet, thirty years earlier.

took David aback. The wild man spoke just two words: 'Tchy-Lama.'

In his surprise the fossil fell from David's lava-covered hands. 'Sambdatchiemda!' he shouted, 'Sambdatchiemda.' The Chinese knew him as 'Tchy-Lama'; the Vincentian Fathers knew him as 'Sambdatchiemda'.

It was April 1866. David was near Erh-shih-san-hao, some 100 miles (160 km) north-west of Peking. It was there he was to pick up Sambdatchiemda, who was to pilot him across Mongolia and the Gobi Desert. The authorities at the Museum of Natural History in Paris had been delighted with the various animal and plant specimens which David had collected on his travels, notably to Jehol two years earlier. Many of these had never been dreamed of, let alone seen, in Europe. Victor Duruy, the Minister of Public Instruction, had commissioned David to undertake a '*mission scientifique*' to the wild and barren regions of Mongolia and the Gobi Desert. Much of this region, like the sandy deserts of the Ala Shan, had never been visited by a European. Even in Peking the region was just a blank on the map. Only in some old manuscripts belonging to some Tibetan lamas was there even perfunctory mention of a few towns in the vast region between the great Yellow River (Hoang-Ho) and the capital Peking.

Sambdatchiemda was a strong, middle-aged Mongolian, a former Buddhist monk who had been converted to Christianity. It was he who, thirty years earlier, had acted as guide to Fathers Huc and Gabet, Vincentian priests like David, on their celebrated journey to the prohibited land of Tibet. They had been among the first missionaries ever to enter its forbidden capital, Lhasa: 'Land of the Spirits'. Not only did they gain access to the famous Buddha-La

(Potala) palace, home of the Dalai Lama, then a mere child of nine, but they managed to stay several months in Lhasa. They finally had to abandon their hope of setting up a Christian mission in the very heart of Buddhism when the Regent gave them the choice of adopting lamaism or of getting out.

There was little doubt that Sambdatchiemda sprang from the feared Dchiahours stock. The Dchiahours hailed from the land of San-chu'an, the 'three valleys'. They possessed in full measure the knavery and cunning of the Chinese without any of their politeness and without their language. They had a language of their own, a medley of Mongol, Chinese and East Tibetan. They claimed to be of Tartar origin – descendants of the redoubtable Genghis Khan, who at one time had conquered an enormous empire embracing China, Tartary, India, Iran, Syria, Poland, Hungary, Austria. The Dchiahours held life cheap; invariably they had a sabre at their side and a long matchlock on their shoulder. For a word, even a look, they would fight and kill one another. A Dchiahour who had never killed anyone was considered to have no right to hold his head up among his countrymen. The man most honoured was the one who had committed the greatest number of murders. Understandably the Dchiahours were held in dread by all their neighbours.

David introduced Sambdatchiemda to Brother Chévrier, who was also to accompany them on the expedition. David had been quite happy to make the journey on his own, but the vicar apostolic had insisted that he should have a companion – Brother Chévrier. The mortality rate among the missionaries was increasing alarmingly: in the past year alone several priests had been murdered.

Brother Chévrier was from the big mission station at Suanhwa, which David had passed through some days earlier. At Suanhwa David had been much impressed by the work of the local women who ran an orphanage – Sainte Enfance – for little children abandoned by their parents because of some infirmity. He met a twelve-year-old girl there who had been tied to a tree in a deserted spot, to die of hunger and exposure, or be devoured by wolves. Her fault was that she had started to go blind. A passing traveller had rescued her and brought her to the home. After some treatment she was slowly beginning to see again.

David's plan was to establish a summer base at Saratsi, and explore the range of mountains that lay 600 miles (965 km) to the west of Peking. However, what he learned about the route was far from encouraging. The Hui-hui, fanatical Muhammadans of the Kansu province, were threatening the region again. A few years previously there had been a Muslim uprising, when the followers of Islam had massacred the Chinese wholesale and sacked their temples. In addition, numerous bands of robbers, not to mention warlords and disaffected generals, with their rag-tag armies, infested the route he hoped to follow. But, as he wrote later, 'it would be necessary to renounce all travelling to distant parts if one had to wait for peace in this Empire, where brigandage and armed rebellion have occurred for so many years'.

5

INTO MONGOLIA

Transportation was a problem. There were no muleteers and any potential porters were not prepared to travel far from their homes, especially as they were needed in the fields to plant oats and potatoes, millet and buckwheat. But, like everywhere else in the world, if the remuneration is tempting enough there will always be people prepared to risk their necks. Eventually David obtained some carters, a wagon and four beasts.

The baggage was considerable. The bedding alone consisted of several covers, since they would be sleeping on the ground, or on bare bricks – if, indeed, they chanced upon an inn. In Mongolia there are only two seasons: nine months of winter and three of summer. While the days were stiflingly hot on the desert steppes, the nights were bitter. Freezing to death was a frequent occurrence among the soldiers guarding the outposts.

In addition there was David's 'house in the desert'. This was a Mongolian tent which he had purchased at Suanhwa, the ancient capital of the Mongol emperors. In Mongolia inns were few and far between, and were little more than stables, just as they had been in biblical times. A tent would make life a little more bearable.

A whip cracked and the small, hooded cart, loaded to the skies, rumbled forward with a screech of its rusty axle. David, Brother Chévrier and Samb-datchiemda were off. Ouang Thomè was staying behind to take care of the numerous specimens of flora and fauna that David had collected on his journey from Peking during the past month. If these were not treated they would succumb not only to the ravages of the weather, but also to the attention of the ubiquitous termites and ants and other sundry insects.

The cart had no springs, and jolted noisily on the uneven terrain as they headed west to cross the vast barren plains of Inner Mongolia. David planned to travel westward to Saratsi, travelling from early morning till seven at night. They took it in turns to sit atop the baggage while the others walked.

Eventually David obtained a wagon, similar to the one shown here,
for his journey into Mongolia, to the mountains 600 miles (1000 km)
to the west of Peking. 'A whip cracked and the small, hooded cart, loaded to the skies,
rumbled forward with a screech of its rusty axle. They travelled every day from
early morning till seven at night. They took it in turns to sit atop
the luggage while the others walked.'

On 4 April they left China. At the village of Hsin-p'ing k'ou they crossed
the Great Wall of China – or what remained of it. '*Wan-li-ch'ang-ch'eng*', 'the
Great Wall of 10,000 *lis*' (3 *li* equal 1 mile – 1.6 km), the Great Wall of China
extended from the westernmost province of Kansu to the Yellow Sea in the
east. It had been constructed in 214 A.D. by the Emperor Tsin-Chi-Hoang-Ti to
keep out the marauding Tartars and Manchus. Far in the distance the earthen
towers of the Wall stood out starkly, sentinel-like, on the slopes of the
mountains to right and left.

Here and there in the surrounding countryside *manis* inscribed on tall
white flags fluttered from buildings. '*Mani*' is an abbreviation of the Buddhist

formula *om mani padme hum*, 'O, the gem in the lotus. Amen'. The words, a Tibetan transcription of a Sanskrit formula, express the desire to acquire perfection in order to be absorbed in the eternal and universal soul of Buddha.

They waved to a wizened old lama, piously whirling the *chukor*, or 'turning prayer', in his right hand. Each revolution of the wheel, on which was inscribed *om mani padme hum*, was as good as the prayer having been recited. The poor fellow was so taken aback at the motley procession going past him that his *chukor* was immobile for several moments.

It was pleasantly cool in the morning, but as the day wore on it became windy, with flurries of snow making the journey unpleasant. The low volcanic mountains were denuded and deforested; the only trees in the barren land were a few poplars and pollarded elms. No trees were ever planted for they would be

The Great Wall of China which extended from the westernmost province of Kansu to the Yellow Sea on the east. The Wall was built in 214 AD by Emperor Tsin-Chi-Hoang-Ti to keep out the marauding Tartars and Manchus.

43

A Mongol tent – David's 'house in the desert'.

pulled up the next day by some poor wretch for fuel.

That evening they used the Mongol tent for the first time. It consisted of rags of felt and goatskin stretched on a wooden frame. Up to a height of about 3 feet (1 m) from the ground it was cylindrical in form; it then became pointed like a conical hat. In addition to the door there was another opening to let out the smoke. This opening could be closed at any time by a piece of felt which fastened above it in the tent and which could be pulled over it by a string which hung by the door.

While he was sharpening his great Russian cutlass on the top of his leather boots, Sambdatchiemda recounted his early days. 'I never killed anyone, but that was merely because I did not stay long enough in my native Three Valleys; for at the age of ten they put me into a great lamasery. I had for my master a very rough, cross man, who gave me the strap every day because I couldn't repeat the prayers he taught me. But it was to no purpose he beat me; I could learn nothing: so he left off teaching me, and sent me out to fetch water and collect fruit. But he continued to thrash me as hard as ever until I at last ran off with some provisions and made for Tartary.'

Before retiring for the night David carefully unwrapped a notebook from its waterproof covering. Even though he had only been in China a relatively short time he had contracted a form of pernicious anaemia. This weakened his memory, which was why he made a special point of recording each day's adventures and misadventures in a diary. Having recorded the events of the day, he said the prayers which replaced the recitation of the breviary for the travelling missionary.

Before long there was nothing to see: no towns, no buildings, no forests, no cultivation. The high plateau extended to nowhere in every direction. A herd of untameable wild asses in the distance was the only decoration of a naked landscape. Above them the occasional crow, eagle or vulture circled in search of some unsuspecting prey. But the striped ground squirrels, recently emerged from their long winter sleep below ground, were alert, standing on their hind legs to better observe the travellers. Red-coated marmots, not so bold, flounced nervously into their burrows at the first hint of danger.

Occasionally the savage and gloomy landscape was broken by a bog or stream; occasionally by rugged and imposing mountains or by yawning ravines that rent the earth. The travellers had to pick their way with circumspection past drab grey gullies. Slowly the ochre earth lost its yellow tint, yielding to white as though covered with snow and they passed several salt-caked bogs. The presence of aquatic birds heralded one of the many 'salt-lakes' peculiar to the region; terns and blackheaded gulls swooped and chattered. They were glad to finally reach a lake, several miles long, its shores frosted with a border of carbonate of soda. A Mongolian eagle swooped down on the teeming ducks, while exotic herons and demoiselle cranes strode majestically with leisurely paces. Birds and ducks feasted on the ends of reeds and the broad leaves of waterlilies. The cries of thousands of birds on the lake made a welcome change after the silence of the desert steppe, where no one spoke, because the ever-present wind made speech inaudible.

There were no boats on the lake. The Mongols had no thought or need for navigation: in winter the lakes were frozen so solid that people could walk and ride over them. In the far distance the gaily coloured roofs of a lamasery rose out of the haze. The lamas survived on the offerings which the pious brought them when the lake was frozen over. David filled a bag with lumps of the freely available salt, for their own use and also for bartering with cameleers on the way, as camels are very fond of salt.

A camel caravan rests in the Koko Nor.

The incongruous expedition snailed its way across the barren wilds of Mongolia. They passed a camel caravan which had stopped for pasturage. The camels, which had not yet shed their winter coats, chewed the colourless tufts of brittle vegetation which camels can eat but which horses cannot. Many of the cameleers, their faces almost black from continuous exposure to the relentless sun, were draped in long goatskins; a few more hardy ones were naked to the waist, their shaggy garments gathered in great unwieldy bunches round their midriffs. Most wore amulets round their necks. Some, astride between the two humps of their Bactrians, like bales of merchandise, slept as soundly and as comfortably as if they were in bed. The tinkling of the bells suspended round the camels' necks made pleasant music.

Each day the wind would get up with unnerving punctuality, mercilessly peppering the expedition and everything around with sand. The dazzling glare and the constant bombardment with grit-laden sand moulded David's eyes into almond slits, like Chinese eyes. The sun blackened his chapped face. He was daily becoming less and less distinguishable from the local inhabitants – a definite advantage.

On the bleak horizon tiny wisps of black smoke swirled out of beehive-shaped tops, which, as they got nearer, began to look like so many inflated balloons about to lift off. They turned out to be Mongol tents with sheep and gazelles grazing nearby. A few women collected dried dung, invaluable as fuel, in their wide skirts; others heaped the dung around the dwellings.

As they approached, a wild-looking Mongol – a big bear of a man, lacking in his native centaur dignity – shambled towards David like some monster. Garbed in a large sheepskin, the wool towards his skin, with one shoulder bare and one hand on the hilt of a fearsome broadsword, he lurched from side to side like a great battleship riding out a storm as he made his ungainly approach. Other Mongols, looking more comfortable on horseback, joined the man who was on foot, their ponies dwarfed by the voluminous sheepskins which cocooned their riders. They all carried a musket or matchlock slung across their backs, and all wore broadswords as well. But their countenance was as deceptive as it was frightening. David and his group were received generously.

Next morning David was surprised to see men, tents and herds all vanish in the twinkling of an eye. The animals having devoured all the grass in the vicinity, the chief gave the signal for departure, and all the shepherds, folding their tents, drove their herds before them in search of new pastures.

In contrast to the Chinese, who were universally sceptical and indifferent in matters of religion, the Mongols were essentially a religious people. The Chinese had plenty of pagodas and kept idols of all sorts and sizes in their homes, but for them religion was limited to these externals. With the

A wild-looking Mongol from Koko Nor.

Mongols, future life meant everything, the things of this world nothing, and they lived in the world as if they regarded themselves as foreigners travelling through life. They seemed driven by some secret power which impelled them to wander unceasingly from place to place, possessing to perfection the qualities of a pastoral and nomadic people. Their senses of sight, hearing and smell were prodigiously developed. The Mongol could hear the trot of a horse at a great distance and detect the scent of distant flocks and the smoke of distant encampments.

The sound of raised, angry voices brought David to a halt. Sambdatchiemda generally had a sour and savage demeanour and a perverse temperament which often made him anything but an agreeable fellow-traveller, but his visage was now wild. He was brandishing the huge Russian cutlass that he had purchased at Tolon-Nor and which always hung from his side.

'It is this way,' one of the carters shouted, pointing to a yawning ravine.

'Barbarian, I know it is this way,' replied Sambdatchiemda, pointing in quite a different direction. To call anyone a barbarian was the lowest form of contempt.

They were lost, and it was now dusk. David's anxiety rose. They should have reached an inn by now. Mongolia was the haunt of a large number of wild animals, of which the ubiquitous hares, marmots, grey squirrels, foxes, lynxes, yellow goats and eagles were of no concern, but the large number of wolves, wild camels, brown and black bears, even yaks, and tigers were. The roar of a wild animal compounded their fears.

'Well, you go your way and I'll go mine,' Sambdatchiemda shouted as he

47

Beehive-shaped Mongolian tents.

waved his cutlass and disappeared into the valley.

The sudden howling of a leopard, coming from the valley into which Sambdatchiemda had descended, terrified them. They all feared the worst. More howlings of strange beasts intensified their concern. Armed with only a sword Sambdatchiemda was no match for a leopard or tiger. At least David had a gun. He sprang up and began the eerie descent into the valley, stumbling in the dark. His eyes strained into the darkness as he started at the breaking of twigs. He put the gun to his shoulder as a large black shadow loomed before him.

'Tchy-Lama?' David called before his finger pressed on the trigger. There was a grunt – from Sambdatchiemda.

It was well after nine o'clock when they reached the village of Cha-p'a-te, which consisted of a few miserable dwellings. The so-called inn was nothing but a stable, but at least it would give some shelter.

The face that greeted them must have been the cruellest in the world. From the white cap that topped his long pigtail David knew that it belonged to a Chinese Muslim. He was a member of the race of fiercest fighters, cruellest pillagers, and stormiest petrels in all of Central Asia. The hard, cunning, cruel face was irate at being disturbed so late; the small bloodshot eyes glittered red in the starlight. No, he had no accommodation, no food, no water, for anyone.

They were finally allowed to shelter only after payment in advance of an exorbitant fee. They were herded into a dirty cabin, not 6 feet (1·8 m) square. As they prepared for the night the innkeeper tried to introduce two bald-headed nuns into their company. David would not stand for that, however, and the group, cramped like tinned sardines, at least spent the night comprising only the male sex. They were so crowded that two unfortunate travellers ended up sleeping with half their bodies outside the door. Next morning the two bodies were covered in snow and almost literally frozen to death, even though it was now spring. Large yellow rats with long black claws scurried over the huddled, heaving chrysalid of human bodies, registering their indignation at the unwarranted invasion of their nocturnal playground. David did not sleep, not only because of the cold and the rats but also on account of the lice that attacked him. He was soon regretting not having adopted Father Huc's anti-lice remedy. This was to mix half an ounce (14 ml) of mercury, divided into little specks as fine as dust, with tea-leaves reduced to a paste by chewing. The mixture was then infused into a string of cotton, loosely twisted, hung round the neck. The theory was that the lice would eat the bait, swell, become red and then die.

The day began even more miserably for David. The carters had decided they had had enough and were turning back. This was understandable. In addition to the constant fear of bandits, the elements plagued them relentlessly and unmercifully. One day they were almost buried alive in an avalanche of sand blowing from the Great Desert of Gobi. On another occasion they were assailed by a hurricane. The wind was the bane of their lives: ubiquitous, inescapable, merciless, following them everywhere; and scourging them constantly. It was enough to drive one mad. Speech was impossible and after a time so was consecutive thought.

David was now left only with Sambdatchiemda and Brother Chévrier. The three of them, with their creaking cart and four skeletons of horses, struggled on against the unpredictable weather and the inhospitable terrain. The poor condition of the horses was causing grave concern: there was no water and the few plants that did occasionally come into view were all shrivelled up. The horses' ribs stuck out starkly from their moth-eaten flanks – unless they could get fodder for them soon the animals would surely die.

The plight of their expedition was brought home to them when they stumbled on human skeletons and the carcasses of animals strewn around – all that remained of luckless caravans that had preceded them. Overhead buzzards circled as they waited impatiently for another meal, and a royal eagle, perched motionless on some high ground, eyed them. In Mongolia no one hunts or molests the eagle; it makes its nest where it pleases and there rears its eaglets and itself grows old without in any way ever being harmed by human beings.

At night they fastened rugs round the bodies of the horses and enveloped their heads in rolls of camel hair to keep them warm and conserve their failing strength.

25 April – David remembered the day, not only because it was the feast of St Mark the Evangelist. That day they had the good fortune to stumble on a small, almost dried-up stream. The water was yellow and brackish, but that did not deter the horses. Some wild dandelions growing near by provided the luxury of a 'salad' with the tasteless *tsamba*.

The brittle ochre earth, heavily eroded, was becoming increasingly streaked with red. Tiny specks of gold glistened in the sand beneath their feet. Presently they passed a group of men, squatting on their haunches, washing the dust for the precious metal. Later they passed a group of shepherds huddled round a fire of argols, busily extracting gold from the dust they had found while tending their herds. More loess hills came into view, their dun-coloured slopes ribbed horizontally with rolling terraces of cultivation.

The sight of men carrying blocks of coal on their backs indicated they were now near the coal-mines of Saratsi. They were nearly 'home'. A lamb peeping biblically out of a boy's sheepskin robe as he trotted demurely past on his donkey heralded peace and a respite from the bandit-infested wilds they had negotiated. They passed a huge, intricate waterwheel, whose proprietor was selling water to the farmers.

On 1 May the expedition caught its first glimpse of the mighty Hoang-Ho or Yellow River, as it bore the vast quantities of sand blown into it from the Alechan Mountains to the Yellow Sea, 1,000 (1,600 km) miles away. On 5 May the travellers finally reached their destination – Saratsi. They had been travelling nearly three weeks.

6

SARATSI

Saratsi was a fairly large town, nestling at the foot of a high mountain with a pointed peak and very steep slopes. Above it stood the lamasery which, it was reputed, the Panchen (or Tashi) Lama, the highest dignitary in Tibet after the Dalai Lama, had once visited. The lamasery was built in Tibetan style: square, two and three storeys high, painted red in parts, whitened with lime in others, and, with its gaudily coloured roofs, forming a rich contrast with the dark Mongol tents and Chinese houses of mud and wattle which clustered round.

At the sight, Sambdatchiemda's usually taciturn expression yielded to undisguised delight: he had lived here as a lama some twenty-five years earlier. He stood and gazed, almost in disbelief, the memories slowly flooding back.

On the surrounding slopes poppies grew in wild profusion. It was from the poppy that opium – ta-yen, or big smoke, also called *Hsi-yang-yen*, European smoke – was extracted.

The three travellers stood back to allow a caravan of carts, laden with bales of opium, creak past them. The bales of precious merchandise were escorted by an escort of fierce soldiers who every now and again cried out at the top of their lungs that they were carrying a precious cargo and challenged anyone to contend with them. Even the bandits would be foolish to take up the challenge, and they seldom did. A person of obvious consequence followed, borne on a litter drawn by four of the famous Kansu mules. He was seeking the shelter of the escorting soldiers.

David was surprised to see so many grey-green faces, the complexion of the opium addict. They, in turn, stared in astonishment at him: they had never before seen a white man. As the expedition approached the town centre more and more curious onlookers flocked to see it. They threaded their way through the long, narrow dirty streets followed by a motley crowd of opium addicts, idlers, thieves and riff-raff of all kinds.

David presented his passport to the authorities. They stared at the

51

A Buddhist lamasery

passport and the Chinese-Mongol certificate signed by the mandarins of Tsung-li Ya-men and Count de Bellonet, the French chargé d'affaires at Peking, sometimes holding the papers the right way up, sometimes upside down. They could not make head or tail of his documents or of David. Was he a Russian spy? Was he searching for gold and silver, which he would steal from the country? Or was he like another white man who had spent his time in China and Tibet making maps? The authorities were highly suspicious of anything or anyone to do with maps, especially after the Moorcroft affair. Moorcroft was an Englishman who had infiltrated into Lhasa in 1826 under the pretext of being a Kashmiri merchant. After a sojourn of twelve years in Lhasa Moorcroft left the capital of Buddhism. But he was assassinated on his way back to Ladakh. Among his effects was found a huge collection of maps, geological charts and sketch plans which he had drawn during his travels in and around Lhasa.

The Indian surveyor and cartographer Pandit Krishna was more fortunate. Code-named A-K, the first and last letters of his name transposed, he survived in the forbidden land for some years without detection. Disguised as a lama, he kept his map-making papers hidden in his *chukor* or prayer-wheel; his Tibetan rosary beads served for counting paces. When the Tibetan authorities found that their neighbouring power, India, was making a secret survey of their country they were furious. God help anyone caught making maps!

Maybe David was another Moorcroft? Father David explained that scientific knowledge was his only motive for his presence there but the authorities remained suspicious. Reluctantly they allowed him to stay, but only for a few days.

The Muslim innkeeper refused to take David in; the price went up and up; he still refused. David decided he would continue living in his tent. They turned the cart and the party began to push its way through the motley crowd of curious onlookers. David was sorry at this turn of events as he had amassed quite a collection of specimens of flora and fauna, most of which were completely unknown to European botanists and zoologists. These all had to be treated, cured, prepared and preserved, and to do this he would need dry, reasonably dust-free conditions. They had not gone far when the Chinese

Muslim came up to say that he might be able to find some accommodation that had suddenly become available. They settled a price, and led their somewhat confused animals back to the inn whence they had come.

When they had tethered their horses in the courtyard, nosebags with barley were provided for the skeletal animals. David took careful note of a mulberry tree in the corner, the fat, white mulberries gently falling to the ground. The room was not large, but it was adequate and would allow him some privacy in his scientific work. He had barely brought the last piece of baggage into the

Opium poppies growing in wild profusion on the slopes surrounding Saratsi.

room, however, when the paper windows were pierced here and there by curious fingers anxious to see what the Westerner was doing. It was obvious the household did not observe the tenets of Islam strictly: the innkeeper smoked, which for a good Muslim is forbidden; the pretty girls – presumably his daughters – were also singularly unmindful of Koranic law, staring and smiling at the infidel quite unashamedly. The innkeeper went by the name of Wang. When he was out of doors he wore his blue turban on his head; when indoors he used it to hold up his trousers.

That night David and Sambdatchiemda enjoyed the luxury of goose egg and onion, and tea with red pepper in it. David was tempted to open a bottle of cognac which he carried with him, but resisted; the brandy was for medicinal purposes in an emergency. Sambdatchiemda partook modestly of the strong, local whisky.

By now the paper windows were so perforated by finger holes as to be useless, both for keeping out the wind and the dust and discouraging the prying eyes. A complaint to the innkeeper solicited some action when some cash entered the discussion, and the windows were boarded up.

The inhabitants of Saratsi seemed divided equally between the Chinese and Mongol races. The entire population, whichever race they belonged to, was obviously addicted to opium. The people were extremely poor, but what little they had was spent on the expensive drug. No one deprived him- or herself of the sensual pleasure it gave. The plight of the children was dreadful. He was not surprised to learn that in the province 40 per cent of children born died before they were one year old. It was a wretched place, where almost every second house seemed to be an opium den. He peeped into one: under the paper Chinese lanterns some individuals were sitting, some lounging, some prostrate, all puffing the weed. A few were outstretched, unconscious, insensible to any pleasure the weed could offer. The big bald-headed proprietor, in black three-quarter-length pantaloons, an open blouse exposing his naked torso, and with no slippers on his feet, invited David to join his 'lotus-eaters'. David declined. The Chinaman could not believe that the Europeans, who had first brought opium to his country, did not smoke the drug.

Before retiring David wrote up his diary, in which he referred to how he was hounded by the authorities. The diary records: 'In response to all these tiring suspicions, which we cannot dispel by words, we show great patience, self-control and artlessness. To survive in China one of the great virtues needed is patience.'

Despite the suspicion and constant surveillance that dogged his every move, David decided to explore the mountains beyond the coalmines.

Sambdatchiemda motioned them to halt. He had his right forefinger pressed against his lips: silence! He pointed ahead to where the brow of the hill protruded into the sky. David could see only the horns; but what horns! This was the notorious *Naemorhedus goral candatus*, the rare antelope he would love to add to his collection. Sambdatchiemda had often hinted he would like to try out David's gun – should he let him try it out? His life might one day depend on Tchy-Lama's skill with the gun. Sambdatchiemda grinned from ear to ear as David handed him the gun. The ex-*bonze* crept forward to get a better aim, David watching him. The report reverberated like a crack of thunder round the hills. The horns disappeared from view. Sambdatchiemda was jubilant, holding the gun aloft. He had got it. They hurried forward, brushing past the thickets, but before they could reach their prize another man, equally fierce and armed as Sambdatchiemda, was shouting abuse and gesticulating frighteningly with his gun. Sambdatchiemda had shot, not the prized *Naemorhedus goral candatus*, but one of the enraged man's rams. Massive compensation saved an ugly situation.

Sambdatchiemda began to load the animal on to the mule, his mouth already watering with the thought of juicy mutton for the next several days.

'Put that down,' the dead animal's owner said in a firm voice. Sambdatchiemda stopped loading, scowling, unaccustomed to being spoken to in such a peremptory manner.

'What do you mean – "Put that down"? The master has just paid you for it,' Sambdatchiemda retorted.

'He paid for the killing of it, not the eating.'

'What do you want with it, anyway? You are a Muslim. You can only eat animals that have been killed by the knife.'

The man was stung by Sambdatchiemda's reminder of his religious obligations. He strode up to the dead ram and cut its throat. 'There you are; it has now been killed by the knife.'

Sambdatchiemda gave him a derisory and disgusted laugh. David began to move away, before Sambdatchiemda lost his temper with the doubly-dead ram's owner. In a voice that was easily audible Sambdatchiemda recited an old proverb about the Chinese Muslims which summed up their attitude to Koranic law: 'Three Muslims are one Muslim, two Muslims are half a Muslim; one Muslim is no Muslim.' They returned to Saratsi without the 'mutton'.

Tchy-Lama was naturally very keen to visit his old lamasery, the more so as he had heard that two compatriots from his native village were lamas there.

On the way up to the monastery David had admired the peak behind it. Once there, he asked if he could climb it. The lamas laughed: impossible! No one could ever get to the summit. David decided, however, that he would try: it was years since he had put his Basque mountain training to any use. Leaving Sambdatchiemda with his cronies he set off. It was not long before he realised the lamas might be right after all: the summit was impregnable. The narrow track that giddily zigzagged up the face of the cliff soon disappeared and the cliff face became almost sheer. He was finding difficulty with his footholds; his grip was becoming dangerous as vertigo and fear brought the sweat to his

An opium den. Under the paper Chinese
lanterns some sat, some lounged and some
were prostrated while puffing the weed.

palms. He gazed uneasily at the almost dried-up river snaking its way hundreds of feet below him. Just as he began another traverse on the cliff-face the block of stone he was clinging to came loose – it was a miracle he had not followed it into the yawning abyss. His nerve shaken, he decided to acknowledge defeat. The lamas were right. But his adventure had not been to no avail, as far as natural history was concerned. As his diary recorded:

> 'In the crevices between these rocks grew Thuya, a *Xylosteum lonicera*, three Spiraea, and a barberry with large leaves. Lower down I find a pretty Cotoneaster in bloom, a stunted spiny *Prunus*, yellow rose bushes, *Caragana*, an elm with large winged fruits, etc. On the steep rocks there is much dung of roe deer, of *Naemorhedus goral candatus*, and of wolves.'

During the night an earthquake shook the town. Next morning a large angry crowd gathered outside the inn, shouting abuse at David: the earthquake was due to the arrival of the foreigners in their midst. David felt it was safer to stay indoors, though the innkeeper was all for ejecting them. David settled down to sort out his collection of plants, animals, butterflies and insects, and interesting rock and fossil specimens. Through the cracks in the boarded window he could see the brown eyes peering back at him through the slits.

The loud banging of a tom-tom summoned the local populace to listen to a proclamation. This increased David's already fuelled anxiety: could it be about him? David and Sambdatchiemda went and stood as inconspicuously as possible at the back of the surging, attentive throng. The proclamation was from the mandarin of Tchang-Kouren, who had come to Saratsi to forbid the planting of the opium poppy and to order the plants already germinated to be pulled up.

The crowd listened for a short while and then dispersed. Everyone knew this was just a ruse by the mandarin who, while paying lip-service to the law, actually gave permission to those cultivators who were prepared to pay him handsome bribes to continue growing the poppies. Despite the prohibitions poppy fields abounded for all to see.

That afternoon David was visited by the authorities. Was he not a foreign spy? What was he doing with all those rocks – was he not prospecting for gold and silver? David patiently tried to explain yet again the purpose of his visit to these far-flung outposts of the Celestial Empire, but the bureaucrats were not convinced.

7
THE MOUNTAINS OF WU-LA-SHAN

David was pleased with the natural history specimens he had so far collected, most of them quite new to him. Now the mountains of Wu-la-shan tempted him, where local hunters went to procure the new antlers of deer. These fetched up to 40 ounces (1·1 kg) of silver a pair when sold to doctors, who used them as part of their *materia medica*. He had also heard of strange new species of plant and animal life that abounded there. A peculiar species of goat, which the locals referred to as *ching-yang*, inhabited the inaccessible rocky ramparts of the mountains. There was also the *ling-yang*, a similar but larger animal highly prized for its white horns which were used medicinally. Argali (the great wild sheep), called *pang-yang* by the Chinese, hid in the highest peaks. In western Wu-la-t'o, where the hills still remain wooded, roe deer and red deer were said to be common. What fascinated David most was the prospect of acquiring the famous blue pheasant, said to be as large as a chicken, with a short black tail, red beak and feet, whose upper parts of the body were blue, the underside dark indigo. Of added interest, especially to Sambdatchiemda, was a monastery renowned throughout all of Wu-la-t'o. Sambdatchiemda had lived there for two years when he was a lama.

Once again, transport was a problem: for such an expedition they needed another animal, but not for any money could David hire one. No one wanted to compromise himself by doing the 'foreigner' a favour. David remembered that Tchy-Lama had friends in the lamasery. He watched as Sambdatchiemda and a worldly old lama repeatedly placed their hands in each other's wide sleeves and by the pressure of their fingers haggled over price. Eventually David was able to hire a donkey at an exorbitant rate.

With 20 pounds (9 kg) of small millet, 10 pounds (4·5 kg) of farina, beans and cooked barley as provisions for an expedition of approximately fifteen days, he and Sambdatchiemda set off for Wu-la-t'o, as David recorded, 'travelling in regions where we take the chance of having no other resources than my

The tributary of the great Hoang-Ho which
had to be forded seventy-two times.

gun. But Sambdatchiemda is a strong Mongol, and, like a Basque, is not easily
rebuffed. So, give us courage!'

Brother Chévrier and Thomè remained behind to guard their 'house' in
Saratsi.

After several hours walking the poor donkey succumbed to its load; it
could go no farther. So Sambdatchiemda, still robust in spite of his fifty years,
loaded his shoulders with 40 lbs (18 kg) and David with 30lbs (13·5 kg). 'This
burden lessens neither our courage nor our cheerfulness, which we need to
execute a laborious and perilous voyage across wild mountains, frequented, it
is said, by brigands and ferocious animals.'

On the way to the village of Chekouen a river (a tributary of the great
Hoang-Ho) had to be forded no less than seventy-two times. That night David
recorded in his diary: 'It never occurs to the Chinese to fix these fords, as could
be done, so one might pass without getting wet. They prefer to go into the
water rather than do some work that would benefit others.'

In Chekouen, a triangular flag flying in front of a house indicated an inn
and eating house. The thought of setting up their tent, collecting dung for fuel,
lighting a fire, cooking their meagre repast, before they could take a rest after

their tiring day did not compare with relaxing and resting in comparative comfort in a warm inn. But the innkeeper, a disagreeable man, with cruel, hawk-like features, busily engaged in drying horse droppings in the courtyard for fuel, refused to take them in. He was more smartly dressed than a Mongol, but just as fierce and barbaric. His turban denoted he was a Muslim. At the best of times the Chinese businessman was a grasping miser, mean, avaricious, with a heart as dry as a ship's biscuit, charging anything up to 40 per cent interest rates, who would not give a traveller even a cup of water except for payment. This innkeeper had further ground for refusing David admission; Europeans were considered evil and dangerous beings. But David was not a man easily deterred. He was firm and was eventually admitted. The light in the room came from an imperfect wick floating in a broken teacup of thick, dirty, stinking oil. David managed to win the confidence of the other occupants of the inn, who finally let him join them to sleep round the *k'ang*, a brick platform under which the smoke of the hearth passed. Here he was thrown in with all kinds of people, smoking, chattering and screaming all night, not to mention the vermin, the fleas and lice: 'the unpleasant little animals which walk about with complete freedom. I shall soon be covered with them; but it is useless to be fastidious here.'

Next morning David managed to kill a grey snake (*Calepeltis*) which still had two yellow rats, whole, in its stomach.

They pressed on with their journey and by evening had reached the famous Lamasery of Five Temples at the foot of a tall mountain at Wu-t'ang-chiao. They pitched their tent a mile below the lamasery, in a place whose aspect was wild and intimidating. Large conifers covered the mountainside; the summit was invisible under a heavy bank of black clouds.

A detachment of lamas came down from the lamasery to see who had intruded on their solitude. They were dressed in yellow or violet robes with red sashes, and on their heads they wore large yellow ceremonial hoods that looked like firemen's helmets. David was informed in no uncertain manner that the Grand Lama was the lord and prince of all the surrounding countryside and that he had better move on. Sambdatchiemda then emerged from the tent. Two of the irate lamas recognised Tchy-Lama and there was much rejoicing. Of course David could stay; the

A *k'ang* or brick platform under which smoke from the hearth passed to provide heat.

Grand Lama himself had given such instructions!

They got little sleep that night. David and Sambdatchiemda had made sure the many squirrel holes under their tent were all carefully blocked up. Even so the ubiquitous rodents made merry around the tent, disturbing even the donkey, which had been brought into the tent because of the presence of wolves. The donkey's presence added enormously to their general discomfort and inconvenience.

The following morning David returned the courtesy visit by the lamas. On his way to the lamasery, through a grove of large willows, he saw about a hundred lamas divided into small groups, seated on the bare ground or crouched on their heels, all shouting at the top of their lungs and pronouncing unintelligible words. These were the lama pupils of the school. Standing in front of each group was the instructor, who, gesticulating like a Chinese comedian, was teaching them to recite by heart Tibetan prayers which he himself did not understand.

Buddhist monks playing chess.

The lamasery was built capriciously in Tibetan fashion. A multitude of small square houses, all washed with white lime, and surmounted by platforms, surrounded the principal temples. Over 1,500 lamas lived here. Several of them crowded round to see the *Kang-jen* or 'white' stranger. They found it hard to believe that other countries besides Mongolia, Tibet, Russia and China existed, or that the sulphur matches, the needles and cotton they used, all came from Europe.

David was pleased to learn that a wild blue fowl, with red feet and bill, did indeed inhabit the highest summits of the mountains, but it was apparently scarce and difficult to catch. An ancient lama recalled that he had once seen the rare bird in the possession of a wood-cutter about twenty-five years earlier. The not-so-ancient lamas professed ignorance.

David and Sambdatchiemda spent much of the day with the lamas, David much taken with a group of monks playing chess. The chessboard was exactly the same as that used in the west; the pieces were differently shaped, but represented the same value and followed the same moves; the rules of the game were just the same. He was surprised to hear one player call 'chik' when he checked a piece and 'mate' when the game ended.

One coterie of lamas was caught by surprise and tried to hide what they had in their hands. They were sniggering over stereoscopic pornographic photographs. Generally, David found the lamas boring and extremely ignorant, especially in matters of history and geography. As for metaphysics, their lack of knowledge was 'incredible', as he wrote in his diary that evening. For many their universe hardly extended beyond their immediate environs.

Sambdatchiemda regarded the present Grand Lama as a false pretender to the office. Years ago the previous Grand Lama, having collected 30,000 *taels* of cash, decided to take it to Lhasa to make an offering to the Dalai Lama, the Living Buddha of Lhasa. With a retinue of lama servants he set off for the Potala. However, two of these men were not happy at seeing the money of Wu-la-t'o going to the much richer chief monastery in Lhasa. At a remote river crossing they beat up the old Grand Lama, hurled him into the river to drown, and absconded with the money.

When news got back to the monastery of Wu-t'ang-chiao that their Grand Lama was dead, the lamas went in search of a young child into whose body the soul of the drowned Grand Lama would have transmigrated. They eventually found a boy endowed with all the signs of the presence of Buddha. The young boy was taken to the lamasery where, in due course, he succeeded as Grand Lama.

Then one day, to the consternation and incredulity of the lamasery, the drowned former Grand Lama was standing at the monastery gates. Several of the lamas fled at the sight of the 'ghost'. Eventually the old man had regained consciousness to find himself prostrate on the bank of the river. He had continued his journey to Lhasa, even though with nothing to offer; and had finally returned to Wu-t'ang-chiao. The former Grand Lama tried to regain his rights. But the new Living Buddha, who was now a very wealthy man, possessing over 1,000 horses, 3,000 cows, a considerable number of camels and sheep, and all the surrounding land, refused to give up his possessions and

61

rights. His lama hangers-on naturally supported him. The old Grand Lama did not press his case at the courts in Kweisui, knowing that, as everywhere in China, the man with money is always right, and he would get no satisfaction. He retired to a small lamasery far away, where he now lived as a simple lama. However, the two men who had attempted to kill him were apprehended and condemned to death.

Next day, David and Sambdatchiemda awoke in a mire; their bedclothes were soaked and their limbs stiff with cold. Despite the fact that it was snowing, they set off, soon standing aside to let a party of pilgrims on their way to the lamasery pass. It was a Mongol princess, being escorted by a troop of mandarins. She was in her middle years, clothed entirely in red cloth. Unlike the mandarins, who laughed heartily at David's shabby turn-out, the lady greeted him with a smile which cheered him immensely.

Although it was summer they frequently encountered heavy falls of snow. The nights were freezing but during the daytime, especially in the valleys, they would be roasted.

Towards late afternoon one day they stopped near some Mongol tents, where they would find water and dung, which they needed to cook their millet. Someone was at the entrance to the tent.

'Who's that?' Sambdatchiemda bellowed.

A female lama, or nun, poked her shaven head into the tent. She was dressed in violet; the female lamas dressed exactly like the men. Women, however, did not become lamas until middle age and after they had brought up their families, and this lady had long since passed middle age. Her broad grin exposing just one or two discoloured teeth, she handed David a pitcher of milk.

'Milk!' David whooped. This was a feast for his eyes: he had not seen milk for months. He and Sambdatchiemda were most grateful. But they both knew that by custom they must give the old lady a present at least equal in value. They had coins, but that was of no use since money had no exchange value for Mongols, who had no use for gold or silver; instead they used bricks of tea or cheap, coloured cloth as legal tender. The two travellers had no other recourse but to dip into their meagre provisions of millet. The lama departed very satisfied.

That evening they feasted, mixing the milk with their sugarless tea and boiled millet. Before retiring for the night David made for the tent entrance. He stepped back in astonishment as a massive bear-like figure blocked his way. The apparition had arrived silently and seemingly from nowhere: a robust, well-built man, Mongolian leather boots just visible below his voluminous goatskin robes. David instinctively stepped back into the tent to within reach of his gun, but it was not needed: the man was begging. The Mongols were great beggars, especially off strangers. This man intoned a long tale of woe: he had lost all his livestock, he was the father of four children, and for the past two days he had had absolutely nothing to eat.

Sambdatchiemda somewhat cruelly brushed him away, but David thought back to the luxury of milk he had just enjoyed. Despite Sambdatchiemda's warnings that they would soon be destitute if they listened to every beggar's plea, David handed the fellow some food. 'I hope someone will give us food when we have none!' Sambdatchiemda said as he pulled his goatskin over him.

That night the rain, wind, snow and the cold, added to the fear of wolves and the barking of wild dogs, ensured no rest. Next morning the tent was completely frozen, so they were obliged to wait till it dried out. Trying to cook their millet with wet, frozen dung was no easy task.

Suddenly David and Sambdatchiemda both stopped what they were doing. The tread of heavy boots grew nearer. Even more unexpected was the voice of a woman singing. David peered out of the tent to see a young girl of about eighteen approaching, her long red dress fastened by a belt which enhanced still further her slim figure. She strode self-assuredly in her high leather boots. Her blonde hair, parted in front, was divided at the back into little braids, their tips fastened at her temples to her toque – a conical hat made of fine pelt and velvet, with a small turned-up brim bedecked with metal jewels and little glass pearls connected to her ear-rings. They exchanged greetings. Unfortunately David's Mongolian was not good enough to keep up a conversation with the girl and Sambdatchiemda was too busy cursing the obstinate dung, which would not burn, to act as interpreter. Disappointed at the seeming impoliteness of the two men the young shepherdess turned away, taking her sheep to drink at the nearby well.

The Yellow River, unhurriedly winding its way down from its source in the mighty Himalayas, was a golden snake in the distance; to the south the low sandy hills of the Ordos country kept sentinel. Kites hovered everywhere; buzzards with enormous claws, Mongolian eagles and royal eagles brooded patiently. Gazelles, their yellow coats matching the yellow terrain, bounded across the plains without fear. David and Tchy-Lama headed for the small rounded hills of yellow earth, their summits formed of very white quartz, giving the effect of snow-covered mountains.

A herd of cows indicated the presence of human beings. But the cowherds fled en masse at the sight of a white man – they had never before set eyes on a European. Or were they, perhaps, some of the many fugitives from justice who haunted the deserted gorges of Wu-la-shan?

As they ascended the pass the wind increased in ferocity. Whenever they could they gathered up dry cow dung and camel dung, which, with the roots and stems of plants, would enable them to make a fire. The wind was now almost a cyclone, and near the summits they had to struggle not to be blown over. They had great difficulty in pitching their tent, even using additional ropes and putting enormous boulders on the twelve staves that held the ropes. The wind blew sand all over their supply of millet and for the rest of their journey their diet was augmented with grains of sand. During the night the wind howled and roared vindictively from the west, the walls of their tent flapping and bulging inwards to ripping point. They tried to sleep under accumulating coverlets of sand.

At daybreak some lamas who had also camped near the summit unbeknown to David came up to congratulate the *Kang-jen* on not having been blown away.

'Where are you going?' one of them asked.

'To western Wu-la-t'o,' David replied.

'Not through the Tatamel gorge?' the lama asked with some concern in his voice.

'Why, yes. How else can we go there?'

'How many of you are there?' David pointed to Sambdatchiemda and the silent, long-suffering donkey, which stood still as Sambdatchiemda piled the baggage on its back.

'Just you two, alone and on foot. Aren't you afraid?' another of the lamas joined in.

'Afraid? Of what?' It was Sambdatchiemda, not boasting, just being his honest self.

'Of what? The brigands, of course. Only yesterday they stripped and murdered two poor lamas who were passing through the gorge on their camels.'

Sambdatchiemda ignored this comment and returned to loading the donkey. David had by now come to realise that a little composure plus the sight of a European face above a beard of several weeks' growth, augmented by the possession of a gun, was sufficient to deter any number of malefactors.

'We are not afraid,' David replied. 'We will go anywhere, in spite of everything.'

The lamas went on their way by no means reassured about the safety of the small group they were leaving behind.

David and Sambdatchiemda came upon a Buddhist altar. This indicated they had reached the highest point of their climb. Before they could take in the spectacular scenery on this side of the pass they stopped and David cocked his gun. Before them, shouting and screaming and gesticulating wildly, were some

Plate 1
Adult male panther.

Plate 2
Rhizomys vestitus, discovered by David near Koko Nor in 1866.

ARNOUL DEL.ET LITH.   ⅕   IMP.BECQUET, PARIS.

Plate 3
Crossoptilon auritum, a pheasant discovered by David in the mountains of Muping.

LÉPIDOPTÈRES RECUEILLIS A MOUPIN, PAR LE R.P. ARMAND DAVID.

1. *Armandia Thaïtina* Blanchard . | 3 a b *Lycœna Cœligena* Oberthür .
2 a b *Pieris Larraldei* Oberthür . | 4 a b *Lycœna Atroguttata* Oberthür .
5 a b *Pieris Davidis* Oberthür .

Plate 4
Some of the many new species of butterfly discovered by David around Muping.

Plate 5
Pteromys albo-rufus, discovered by David in the Muping region in 1869.

Plate 6
Rhinolophus larvatus (adult female – top) and *Vespertilio moupinensis* (bottom),
two species of bats discovered by David in Muping.

Plate 7
Putorius davidianus discovered by David in Kiangsi in 1869.

Plate 8
Macacus tibetanus, discovered by David in the mountainous region of Muping.

Plate 9
Uropsilus soricipes (top) and *Mus chevrieri* (centre) – both discovered by David in the Muping
region – and *Mus ouang-thomè* (bottom). *Mus chevrieri* is named in honour of Brother Chévrier who
accompanied David in his first long journey of exploration to Mongolia, and *Mus ouang-thomè*
after the Chinese helper who accompanied David on his first two long journeys of exploration.

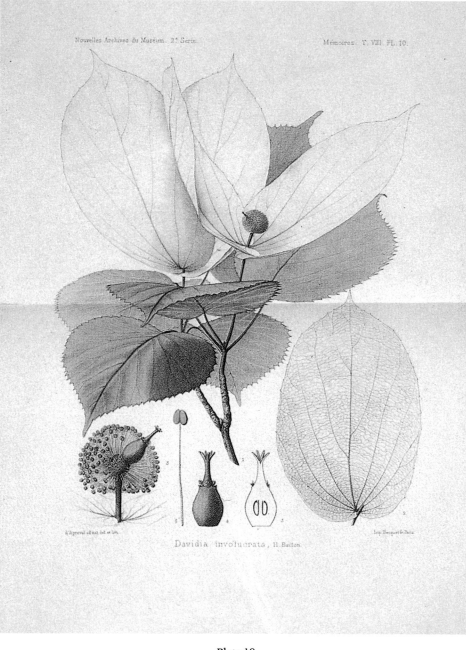

Davidia involucrata, H. Baillon.

Plate 10
Davidia involucrata.

Plate 11
Siphneus armandii, discovered by David in the high Mongolian Plateau in 1866.

Plate 12
A male antelope (*naemorhedus*), discovered by David in the mountainous region of eastern Tibet in 1869.

This is the first scientific portrait of the giant panda (a female), discovered by David in March 1869 in the mountainous region of Muping, eastern Tibet. *Ailuropoda melanoleucus* was A. Milne-Edwardes's scientific name for the animal, and *Ursus melanoleucus* David's name for it.

Elaphurus davidianus (Père David's deer). An adult female and young female (about two years old) obtained by David after 'negotiations' with the guards in the Imperial Hunting Park, Peking, in 1866.

Plate 15
Rhinopithecus roxellanae, discovered by David in the mountainous region of eastern Tibet.
This is an adult female.

ARNOUL DEL. ET LITH.   IMP. BECQUET, PARIS.

PYRGILAUDA DAVIDI.

Plate 16
Pyrgilauder davidi.

SYRNIUM DAVIDI.

ARNOUL DEL. ET LITH. 1/4 IMP. BECQUET, PARIS.

Plate 17
Syrnium davidi.

Plate 18
Dipus annulatus, discovered by David in the salt plains of Mongolia in 1866.

Plate 19
Sciurus davidianus, discovered by David in the mountainous region north-west of Peking. 1866.

PROPASSER DAVIDIANUS.

Plate 20
Propasser davidianus.

of the brigands they had been warned against. David shouted to them to stop, but they continued to hurry towards him. He pointed his gun, then saw that the four men were unarmed. They rushed towards David and Sambdatchiemda in obvious distress.

'Our camels! Our camels! Have you seen our camels?', the first of the men to reach them kept shouting. Evidently they had suffered the full ferocity of the hurricane, and the gales had dispersed their camels they knew not where.

No, they had not seen the camels, Sambdatchiemda replied sympathetically, but they would keep an eye out for them.

Slowly they wound their way to the yellow sandy plains below them. The gorge narrowed almost to a point, so that only one person at a time could pass. The thick, tall shrubs pressed in on them. David spied a magnificent falcon, but had to ignore it; the defile was no place for dallying.

'He must have had too much of the sun,' David thought to himself as he listened to Sambdatchiemda talking to himself. He had fallen into that habit himself. He waited for Sambdatchiemda to come round the corner and catch him up, but Sambdatchiemda did not appear. David could not see him, but could hear him quite distinctly.

'No, I am not alone,' he could hear Sambdatchiemda saying. David stopped to listen. 'There are two of us.'

Another voice was addressing Sambdatchiemda in excellent Mongolian. David turned back to join his companion. A large man, with an imposing red moustache and large, almost aquiline nose, had accosted Sambdatchiemda. He had both hands on his gun, and seemed singularly well-dressed for that barren wilderness.

Sambdatchiemda was simple, but by no means stupid. Like David he had come to the conclusion that this fierce figure was assuredly a bandit. 'There are two of us here,' Sambdatchiemda was saying, 'but there are others in our party; the rest are following close behind. Just wait and you'll meet them.'

The stranger was discomforted at seeing David who, with a two-week-old beard, looked just as wild as anyone in the region.

'I can see you're a hunter. You have your gun ready,' David said in Chinese. The man replied in impeccable mandarin that he was a local hunter.

'I'm so glad we've met you. Tell me about the famous blue pheasant.' The man obviously did not know what David was talking about. 'And what about the *ching-yang* and the *ling-yang* and the *pang-yang*?' David tested him further. The man's fluent speech turned into an incoherent mumble. He was obviously no local, and no hunter, either.

Sambdatchiemda was pointing. There, in a curve of the valley, they could

65

see five horses and two camels, grazing quietly beside two tents.

'Whose horses are they?' David asked.

'Ours.'

'How many are there of you?'

'Five.' It was five horsemen who had murdered the two lamas on their camels. Before David could question the stranger further the man had vanished into the dense thicket as mysteriously as he had appeared.

The oppressive gorge eventually opened its jaws reluctantly. A stream and good grass for the donkey decided their resting-place for the night, although they had earlier decided they could not risk setting up shelter for the night in the deserted gorges, because of brigands and wild animals. They pitched the tent out of sight of the brigands and Sambdatchiemda spread out what provisions remained. They had only three days' supply of millet and *tsamba* left. They must get back to Saratsi by the quickest route – except that the brigands were encamped between them and Saratsi.

David determined to find out more about his neighbours. Leaving Sambdatchiemda to prepare camp for the night, he set off down the steep slopes. In addition to his gun he carried his four-shot revolver. 'The sight of these arms will make a salutary impression on these brigands. I'll go and show them.' Cautiously he scrambled over rocks of granite bearing large crystals of rose-coloured felspar. Small garnets could be seen among the quartz stones, gneiss and mica schists. He pocketed an unusual octagonal crystal of oxidised iron, and descended into the river bed. The strange round-headed lizards did not scamper away as he passed them. David picked out the tracks of roe deer and also, less comfortingly, of wolves. A black stork fished hopefully for what food there was.

When David finally reached the bandits' campsite all that remained of it was a still-smouldering fire and the remains of an unfinished meal of wild onions. He collected up the onions, which would make a pleasant change to their regular diet of millet and *tsamba*.

They were camped in a wild place, surrounded by steep mountains covered with shrubs. All that remained of the forests was a scattering of *Pinus thunbergii*. David deplored the destruction of plants – and animals – that had been carried out haphazardly over the past centuries. In his diary he wrote:

> It is really a pity that the education of the human species did not develop in time to save the irremediable destruction of so many species which the Creator placed on our earth to live beside man, not merely for beauty but also to fulfil an important role in the economy of the whole.

66

There was little sleep that night. An attack by the five bandits was more than a possibility; even more alarming was the howling of a leopard. The strange cries got nearer: David fired a shot. That stayed the howls – for a time. The next morning, arming himself with his gun and revolver, David made for the copse from which the cries were coming. But he heard and saw nothing.

They had to delay their start after David had discovered that both he and his clothes were covered in the large red ticks which infest animals. The itching was unbearable. He must have picked up the ticks while walking through the thicket where roe deer had passed or while he was camped near Mongol animals. He wrote in his diary:

> These parasites are very vigorous; not only do their bites hurt,
> but they force themselves completely into the flesh, from
> which it is almost impossible to pull them out. They die there
> and produce an inflammation which lasts several days.

He recalled the letter he had written to his Superior fifteen years earlier begging to be sent to the missions: 'My desire to go to the missions is motivated in part by a desire to do penance.' He was doing his penance alright.

The travellers' spirits rose when, in the distance, the city of Paotow came into view. It was vindictively hot. Despite the suffocating heat which hit them like a wind, their footsteps quickened over the clayey, yellow and blue soil. The surrounding lands seemed fertile but poorly cultivated. As they got nearer the city, however, their excitement abated. There must have been at least 3,000 soldiers camped inside large squares surrounded by earthern walls. The fear of the rebel Hui-hui from Ning-thia-fou had necessitated a military garrison being established in front of the city. David and Sambdatchiemda joined an ever-increasing throng of refugees fleeing from the rebellious Muslims who had already captured the city of Che-choni-dze. The Tartar soldiers were rudely turning away all travellers, whether they were refugees or not. Like the others, David was rudely refused entry into Paotow.

The following morning they determined once again to enter the city, which extended for about two miles from east to west. Over ten thousand families lived there. The poppy fields that grew everywhere accounted for the increasing signs of deprivation among the population.

Brazenly David and Sambdatchiemda, with their donkey in tow, marched through the camp. The soldiers, mesmerised at the sight of a foreigner walking through their camp, coming from the direction of the rebels, just stood and stared. David and Tchy-Lama and the donkey pushed forward past the gaping soldiery. By now they had entered the city. Some of the more influential refugees who had been refused entry also stood patiently, wondering what special power or influence this strange Westerner commanded.

'Stop! Stop!' David could hear people shouting behind him. But he carried on resolutely. 'Stop! Stop!'

He was obliged to stop finally when his path was physically blocked by a group of Tartar soldiers, their long guns at the ready. By now David and Sambdatchiemda were well into the city.

'The great man, the general, says you must see him,' said one of the soldiers. By now the storm which the suffocating heat of the last few days had portended was beginning to break.

'Why did you let me go past when I was prepared to show him my papers? I have gone too far by now and bad weather is threatening. I have a long way to go before nightfall, and besides I am too poorly dressed to present myself before the great man.'

'We must carry out the orders of the general.'

Tartar soldiers.

After weeks of being pushed around David had reached the end of his tether. He decided toughness, not servility, was the wisest course. He knew, too, that if he gave in and went before the mandarin, he would be subjected to all sorts of questioning, that his pasteboard boxes and bottles filled with all sorts of specimens of flora and fauna would be searched and handled roughly and would be confiscated, and he would be left to rot in prison, despite having valid papers from the highest authorities in the empire.

Sambdatchiemda was alarmed by the anger, sternness and severity with which David loudly told the soldiers that he would not retrace his steps: 'Look here, I am not a soldier subject to your general. I am prepared to observe the rules, but you must also observe them yourselves; that is how it is done in Europe. Do you know who I am?' There was a stunned silence. 'So,'

David continued, 'if you do not know who I am, ask to see my passport, and that is the end of the matter. Is this a country full of savages?' These last words embarrassed those present, who were constantly increasing in number.

'But we do not know how to read,' replied the poor soldiers, 'and our great man wants to see you himself.'

'Well, let him come here then. I am exhausted and I am not going back. What is more, I am a Frenchman and a man of honour.'

A soldier seized David by the arm. 'You must come back to our general.'

'No,' David shouted as he angrily pulled himself away from the offending soldier. Sambdatchiemda, meanwhile, for once a little intimidated by the sight of so many soldiers — they now numbered well over a hundred — fumbled around in search of the precious red bag in which David kept his passport.

'Here,' David exclaimed in a loud voice once the passport had been found, in Mongol and in Chinese, 'here is my *piao*. Show it to your great man. I shall wait for you here. I give you one quarter of an hour to return.' After some hesitation the soldiers departed with the *piao*. By now a huge congregation had collected, staring open-eyed at the foreigner. David was concerned, not for his own safety, but whether he would ever see his *piao* again. Without that his travels would be over.

The crowd broke ranks to let the soldiers through. They were quite out of breath and seemed very surprised to find that David had not tried to escape. David was handed back his *piao*. 'The great man said that you can continue on your journey.'

'That's good,' David replied coolly. Looking at his watch he said, 'One minute still remains of the quarter-hour I gave you.'

The poor soldiers, having lost all their bravado, departed like whipped children. David felt sorry for them; by and large the lot of Mongolian soldiers was a wretched one. All men, whatever their age or circumstances, were obliged to carry arms whenever their chief required them to, and once in the army they had to feed and clothe themselves at their own expense. Rich men were able to bribe the mandarins so that they served near their homes, but the poor were sent far afield, where they often resorted to plunder and brigandage just to subsist.

David and Sambdatchiemda somehow managed to disengage themselves from the crowd of people who surrounded them, and made their way through long dirty smelly streets of opium smokers and idlers. By now large drops of rain had given way to hail. The white pebbles pelted down in sheets. A kindly Chinese shopkeeper invited them into his shop, where they were glad to shelter from the torrential downpour.

It had been an emotionally exhausting day; David would have gladly just

69

fallen asleep, but the strong discipline he had learnt as a young seminarian sustained him. He recounted in his diary his confrontation with the Tartar soldiers, ending: 'Often in this country you must assume a commanding attitude or else you will be crushed. Unfortunately such a role is quite contrary to my nature.'

They continued their journey back to Saratsi by way of the Yellow River, spending that night in their tent, which they pitched in the courtyard of a makeshift inn-stable. The wind blew the smell of human manure, used for cultivation of vegetables, and the whiff of rotting corpses into their tent. They slept on a bed of dried manure and stones, 'which are by no means soft'. He closed his diary for the day: 'I am used to everything'.

Many rumours of the imminent approach of the Muslim rebels reached them, but David and Sambdatchiemda never had the misfortune of confronting the rebels. It was the middle of June and very hot – 124°F (41°C) in the afternoon. They were soon pleased to see in the distance the poppy fields of Saratsi, whose poppies were beginning to open their beautiful, infinitely varied flowers. But, alas, the wheat and barley fields had not prospered so well: the drought had killed them.

David's diary for that night recorded:

> 10 June 1866. On reviewing the incidents of my voyage I am almost astonished myself at my courage. They tell me that it was imprudent to get involved thus in so many dangers and fatigues. I agree; but I answer that in this country good results can be obtained only by surmounting great difficulties.

8

IN SEARCH OF
THE BLUE PHEASANT

David had been told of a forest in western Wu-la-t'o that was reputed to be six hundred miles in circumference, and the largest in the Empire. All kinds of strange animals and exotic plants were to be found there; surely the elusive blue pheasant would also be present. David decided that before returning to Peking he would explore part of this region, which had not been visited by any foreign naturalist before. Finding transportation in Saratsi again proved a problem. Finally, one very hot, sunny day Sambdatchiemda brought news that a lama had agreed to rent his camel, at an exorbitant fee.

The camel is the perfect animal for travel in the desert. However barren the land, it can always find something to eat – even briars and thorns, or dry wood itself, which no other animal will touch. If the soil is impregnated with salt or nitre so much the better. It can go a whole fortnight without eating or drinking. An ordinary load for a camel is 700–800 pounds (320–360 kg), which it can carry 10 leagues (22 km) a day. Provided it is allowed a short holiday occasionally for pasturing it will render service for up to fifty years. The only drawbacks are its heavy, ungracious movements, which take some getting used to, and the excessive stench of its breath, which one never gets used to.

Sambdatchiemda, who was accompanying David and Chévrier on this journey as a guide, cook, interpreter and camel-driver, shouted 'Sok! Sok!' but the camel refused to kneel. This was the season when camels were allowed to graze at liberty on the plains of Mongolia, and this camel was not going to miss its vacation if it could possibly avoid doing so. Finally, with the assistance of the lama they were able to rope its legs and get it to kneel. To the sound of the angry bellows of the camel the lama and Sambdatchiemda finally succeeded in lashing the boxes and sacks on to the straw-stuffed packsaddles which squeezed the humps on either side. They hoped to be away for between fifteen and twenty days, and their provisions included 40 pounds (18 kg) of small millet, 20 pounds (9 kg) of *tsamba*, 3 pounds (1·3 kg) of pork fat and a bottle of

71

Chinese brandy for any emergency.

It was the last day of June 1866. The travellers made their way out of Saratsi early in the morning so as to attract less attention. Brother Chévrier allowed David to walk at his left, the place of honour in China, while Sambdatchiemda led the surly uncooperative camel by a headrope fastened to a wooden pin through its nose, the baggage piled high between its two humps. The camel, loaded and walking at its normal stately unhurried pace, marches at about two and a half miles (4 km) an hour, so it was quite easy to keep up with; the only snag is that the camel never stops, so you have to keep going all the time or run to catch it up later.

The Yellow River, now about 1,600 feet (490m) wide, wound its way slowly through the wide plain, here and there showing evidence of where the banks had crumbled away, adding further to the yellow, muddy appearance of the water. Towards evening a downpour of rain caught them. Thirsty and hungry, and now extremely wet, they sought temporary refuge from the pelting rain in an isolated house, but a nobleman standing in the doorway brusquely turned them away. They begged to have a little millet cooked for them; they would pay for this service. But they were left to soak in the pouring rain. Hardly a promising start – Sambdatchiemda's epithet was unrepeatable.

They continued on their way till they reached a little inn, or rather caravanserai, at Gartchin-yao, where they set up their tent beside the highway. To save on their provisions they entered the inn and ordered a bowl of buckwheat each. Most of the faces staring at them were unusually red – the legacy of opium. Many of the inhabitants were asleep and snoring; those who were not yet in a drugged stupor from the debilitating opium stared wide-eyed at the two white men. Pipes, inviting them to partake of the drug, were offered; the innkeeper expressed surprise at his hospitality not being accepted.

They had little peace that night. Not only did the local populace flock around to stare at the strange white men, but Tartar soldiers obviously with nothing better to do, kept riding up repeatedly to size them up. To make the aggravation complete two mastiffs bayed at the moon for hour after hour.

Their journey took them across a sandy desert plain where they were glad they had a camel for their baggage: a horse's or a donkey's hoofs would have had much less purchase on the sand than the large feet of the camel. Finding water soon became a problem: they had not seen any for some days. However, as David later recorded in his diary, 'Providence provides the remedy alongside the evil'. Between the clumps of cactus and scrub he spotted some liquorice bushes. They sat and drank the black juice from the roots. In the distance the small party could see the far-off hills that would offer them more pleasant travelling than the semi-desert.

The waterless desert plain where David,
Chévrier and Sambdatchiemda drank the
black juice from the roots of liquorice bushes.

They made their way steadily up the gorge at the head of the wide valley
of Merghen. To the left a crystal-clear stream, with the occasional gudgeon
leaping up from it, rushed down to lose itself among the boulders and pebbles
of granite. It was a truly beautiful scene. In his mind David noted the varieties
of vegetation they were passing – the ubiquitous thuya or common pine,
junipers, elms, aspens, birches, poplars and willows. Hosts of brown hairy
caterpillars were busily despoiling the foliage of the smaller shrubs. His
scramble up the rocks to examine an almost inaccessible mulberry tree proved
highly successful: there were the silkworms feeding on the green leaves.

David paused in his collecting of plant and animal specimens: it was
some time since he had seen or heard Sambdatchiemda. The latter had been
sulking all day, as he always did when he did not get his own way. Leading the
camel which carried all their precious belongings, he had deliberately been
lagging behind. This was not a prudent way of showing his displeasure,
however, as the region abounded with bandits.

By now it was getting dark. The two European men retraced their way
down the gorge in search of Sambdatchiemda, but there was no sign of him.
First Chévrier, and then David, shouted out: 'Tchy-Lama! Sambdatchiemda!'

But there was no response. They shouted again but their voices were lost, mingling with the noise of the stream bounding and bubbling over the rocks. They were now truly alarmed.

'Something has happened: he must have had an accident. Or the brigands have got him – and all our precious equipment.' Similar thoughts went through David's mind. Again they shouted. A frightened lark flew out from the bushes near them, a roebuck bounded away in fright, but there was no answer from Sambdatchiemda.

'We must go after him. We *must* find him.' But go where? In which direction?

'You go that way,' said David, pointing towards the path they had used earlier. 'I'll go this way.' The two men parted, agreeing to meet at the same place within the hour.

David had been waiting for well over an hour now at the foot of the gorge. He had not seen or heard anyone, not even Brother Chévrier. Again he resorted to shouting. 'Chévrier! Tchy-Lama! Sambdatchiemda!' he bellowed in his loudest Basque voice. And again. But there was no response from either.

David waited a while longer, and then took his gun from his shoulder. He did not have to load it, knowing from past experience that it was wise always to have a bullet ready in the breech of his gun. He released the safety-catch, pointed the rifle skyward and fired. The shot reverberated through the defiles. He waited: Brother Chévrier would surely fire a shot in reply, but only the rat-ta-tat-tat of the cicadas broke the silence. He fired another shot, and again there was no reply.

It was now dusk. The situation had become desperate. He could not sit there all night; what was he to do? In desperation he started walking along the valley, stopping as his keen hunter's eye picked out the footprints of a camel in the dust. Camels were hardly ever used in these parts, so the imprints in the sand must be those of their camel. He quickened his pace as he followed the footprints, which would sometimes die away and then just as suddenly reappear. He paused to catch his breath.

So Tchy-Lama was heading north with the camel! Lagging behind sulkily he had obviously passed the spot where David and Brother Chévrier had turned off without seeing them and had continued to head north for the summit by a different route. David was bathed in sweat: all three of them were now in desperate situations. Tchy-Lama was somewhere out towards the north, un-armed, except for the Russian cutlass he proudly carried at his side. But this would prove of little use against bandits armed with rifles and on horseback, who would dearly love to capture the camel with its precious cargo. Brother Chévrier was in the opposite direction – south. At least he was armed. And,

74

here was he, in between, and helpless.

David continued following the camel footprints until the darkening gloom made that impossible. He stumbled now and again in the dusk, half-walking, half-running in the hope of catching up with Tchy-Lama. Tiredness made him pause for breath. In a last desperate bid to reach Sambdatchiemda he shouted – almost screamed – aloud: 'Tchy-Lama! Sambdatchiemda!' Only silence responded.

He checked his pace at the sound from in front of him. He could just make out the silhouette of a camel lolloping towards him. And then Sambdatchiemda came into view. The relief in David's heart was immense. Sambdatchiemda's relief was hidden behind a scowling, angry face – angry at having been deserted by his two European companions, or so he asserted.

The two began making their way towards where they thought Brother Chévrier could be. As the darkness closed in, their footsteps gained an added pace of urgency, but along the way the camel held them up on occasions as its large bulk tried to circumambulate obstacles that the two men could skip or scramble over.

David feared that some terrible calamity had befallen Brother Chévrier: perhaps he had fallen into one of the many well-camouflaged traps ingeniously devised to catch wild animals. This was one of the many hazards that constantly plagued the unwary traveller in these regions. Just such a trap had nearly claimed the life of the British naturalist, Robert Fortune, who had fallen into one near Ningpo. He had saved his life by miraculously holding on to a twig as he fell. David Douglas, another British naturalist, had not been so fortunate: he had been gored and trampled to death when he fell into one of those infernal pits. At the appointed rendezvous the two men sat down, and prayed. They were both soon on their feet: the growls of leopards and the bark of wolves added to their alarm.

'Armand! Armand!' It was the voice of Brother Chévrier. There was no time for explanations. The three of them made for what they hoped would be a safer habitation for the night.

The following evening a violent storm jarred their equanimity with alarming thunderclaps echoing in the thousand valleys surrounding them. That night's diary recorded: 'It would be magnificent if there were no danger, but the lightning strikes exceedingly close and hits several nearby rocks.'

On 6 July they came upon a region of rounded hills covered with lovely meadows, reminiscent of the cool, subalpine mountains of Europe. The yellow amarylis, red lily, meadow rue and lily of the valley were here in abundance, and the scent of juniper filled the air. Mongol mustangs ran wild in the enticing fields. A clump of willows heralded water. This would be their resting

The sheer sides of the gorges and narrow track made the descent from the plateau a hazardous venture.

spot for the night. If it was not safe from bandits, at least it was comfortable.

David almost knocked Brother Chévrier over as he suddenly rushed to the river's edge. But he was too late: the large black snake he had seen in the water disappeared into the bushes before he could reach it. This was a disappointment to David; his natural history collection was low on snakes.

Soon afterwards they reached a very high plateau. Below them stretched the plains of the land of the Ordos, crossed by a broad band of yellowish sand. Collecting plants and animals became difficult for David as he tried to protect himself from the swarms of yellow horseflies that attacked him, twenty at a time and with painful bites. The descent from the plateau turned out to be yet another hazardous venture. Not used to the steep slopes of the gorges, the camel had great difficulty in carrying the baggage. The load fell over its head several times, to the detriment not only of the camel but also of the contents. They were obliged to repack and reload everything no less than eight times in a matter of hours – each time experiencing increasing difficulty in keeping the intractable, incessantly grumbling animal on its knees so that it could be reloaded.

Sambdatchiemda lost his bearings. They were not sure where they were or in which direction they should head for Baroutaba. They waited patiently for an old lama, far in the distance, to catch them up. He was one of the itinerant lamas that one met in the most unsuspected places. He belonged to a class of lamas who lived neither in lamaseries nor at home with their families;

they were birds of passage who wandered any and everywhere, subsisting on the hospitality which they knew they would always receive. If they thought fit to sleep where they were they did just that, stretching themselves on the floor and reposing till morning. Next day they would stand at the entrance of their tent, if they had one, watch the clouds for a while, then sally forth, east or west, north or south, no matter where, wherever their fancy or a smoother path beckoned them.

The lama was wearing the familiar sheepskin robe, gathered round his waist by a sash, above which, concealing it, capacious folds overhung, forming a pocket for his few personal possessions. From the folds he produced a wooden bowl. David gave him some food, for which the old fellow was most profuse in his thanks.

'Where are we?' Tchy-Lama asked him, but the lama obviously did not understand. Tchy-Lama repeated the question. The old man dug deep into his scarlet robes and from the pouch pulled out something which he secreted in his clenched fist. Slowly he lowered himself to the ground. Then, with loud incantations to assist his clairvoyance, he threw a dice on to some sand that he had carefully levelled with his hands.

Sambdatchiemda pointed to his temple with his forefinger. David agreed; the old man was obviously mad.

Fortunately a young Mongol soon passed that way, who was able to give Tchy-Lama the information he requested. David, Chévrier and Sambdatchiemda set off in the direction pointed out to them. The old lama tried desperately to keep up with them, but slowly he fell farther and farther behind till he finally disappeared from view.

They pressed on, sometimes covering more than 36 miles (58 km) in a day, under the blazing sun, in a sandy plain where the white earth reflected the heat. From the dunes writhing, golden snakes of sand licked out across the ochre desert. The further they went the more dead carcasses they passed, many of which were of cows which had succumbed to the annual epizootic diseases which take a heavy toll of the horned cattle. Here and there, in addition to the carcasses of cows, were those of horses and mules – victims of wolves and leopards.

Brother Chévrier was finding the going very tough. Whenever the road was flat he would attach himself to the camel and let himself be dragged along to spare himself further fatigue. One day, however, he jerked the rope he was holding too hard, the rope broke and he was lucky to miss the camel's flailing hoof as he made contact with the hard ground, his feet pointing skyward. The incident provided David and Sambdatchiemda with considerable amusement for the rest of the day.

Water was again becoming a serious problem for them: they had not seen any for two days. On the third day they were lucky to find a well. The Tartar Mongols used a primitive but none the less effective way of raising water from wells. A goatskin pail attached to a long rope made of camel's hair was lowered into the water, and the other end of the rope was attached to the saddle of a horse. As the rider rode off the pail was hauled up. David used this method successfully with the camel instead of a horse, but the muddy water he raised also contained frogs, some living, some dead. Fortunately, they stumbled on another well which contained water with which they could make tea and wet the tasteless *tsamba*.

The camel, too, had had enough. The long-suffering beast decided that it would no longer put up with Sambdatchiemda's treatment nor with the swarms of horseflies that were literally drinking its blood, and bolted across the plain. This was disaster! The camel was carrying all their provisions, not to mention David's prized natural history specimens. They spent a whole anxious, tiring afternoon trying to catch it. Tchy-Lama kept running and shouting after the elusive animal, and so did David. But all to no avail. They ran miles, David making sure he kept the animal in his sights. As a last resort he would shoot it, just to get back their provisions. Perhaps the camel sensed this, for eventually it let its frantic master grab its reins. It stood still, wearing that air of dignity associated with defeat. David's relief was beyond words; his precious collection saved — but not for long. Continuous claps of thunder exploded over their heads. The rain came down, not in drops, but in torrents.

They passed an abandoned field which, the previous year, had been the scene of a bloody combat between the Mongols and the Chinese. In their usual expansionist plans the industrious Chinese had begun to take possession of the uncultivated Mongol lands and to cultivate them as their property.

That night the rain-water provided the only seasoning for their insipid *tsamba*, which David was finding increasingly difficult to swallow, mingled as it was with sand and grit. They 'dined grittily', as he recorded in his diary. But if the supper was not satisfying, the night was even worse. Though the tent was fast and the rain had diminished, everything was more or less wet inside, leaving only a small dry corner for the three of them to crouch in, very uncomfortably. Sadly, he also recorded the loss of some of his precious specimens:

> I try above all to preserve my collections, the fruits of unbeliev-
> able hardships. The herbarium specimens are saved, but the
> boxes of insects and other things are damaged considerably and
> irreplaceably.

78

'Sok! Sok!' Sambdatchiemda cried out and the camel knelt obediently beside him, so closing up the entrance to their tent. The region was celebrated for its thieves, who would creep into a traveller's tent and with consummate skill remove everything of value. Even in broad daylight their skill and ingenuity in stealing took some surpassing. But the camel ensured that no intruder would enter the tent. At the slightest disturbance it would let out a cry loud enough to awaken the heaviest sleeper – not that they were able to sleep.

In his diary for 14 July Father David wrote:

> Naturally we have not been able to sleep. We are numb with damp and coldness, but day comes, and, after our usual prayers, which are always our first and last acts of the day, we try to straighten ourselves out.

They waited and waited for Sambdatchiemda to return. David had sent him to purchase some water and dung from a near-by tent so as to prepare the meagre breakfast. He was thirsty and famished, having eaten very little the day before. But there was no sign of Sambdatchiemda. This was Sambdatchiemda's petty vengeance on David for not having earlier taken a road past some of Sambdatchiemda's Mongol acquaintances. When Sambdatchiemda did eventually return, he had obviously eaten very well, but by then it was late and so David and Brother Chévrier began the day's long march without any breakfast, simple as that was.

One night in mid-July David was writing his diary.

'Greetings, brother lama!' David listened as the stranger and Sambdatchiemda exchanged pleasantries.

'How many of you are there?' the stranger asked. This was the give-away question. David sensed at once that their visitor was one of a group of bandits, and cocked his gun. The unexpected sight of a European face, bearded and silhouetted in the light of a dung fire, was too much for the stranger. He vanished into the darkness. David stepped outside. The camel gleamed like some silver wraith in the moonlight. He was surprised that it had not given them warning of the stranger's arrival. That night he kept his gun handy, in case of unwelcome guests.

The next day, while they were resting, a group of Tartar horsemen drew up and surrounded them. David was in no mood for a violent confrontation. For the past few days he had suffered from rheumatism and violent toothache: there were no dentists in the Gobi! He was physically and mentally exhausted. The incessant camping and sleeping in damp places had caught up with his health. Often they would pass the night in the depths of some ravine, or shelter beneath a rock, but the raucous cries of the roe deer and the attention of bandits and strangers made sleeping difficult. Though it was summer, they frequently encountered heavy falls of snow; the nights were freezing but during the daytime, especially in the valleys, they would be roasted. Samb-datchiemda, whose health and strength had been slowly eroded by dysentery, also looked anything but the fierce wild Dchiahour warrior he was. And the poor camel was in worse physical shape than any of them.

David listened resignedly to the conversation. They did not want 'venerable brother's' money or camel or life. Well, that was encouraging. Indeed, they were being friendly.

He was disappointed at not having found the elusive blue pheasant, the whole object of the arduous journey, but he knew that their health was too poor to continue. They had to go back to Saratsi.

On 17 July they entered Saratsi. In the poppy fields the peasants were collecting the opium. The streets were a quagmire of filth. The camel could only get through by fits and starts: a stumble, a jump, another stumble. But at least they were home. He had not found the blue pheasant, but he had found many interesting species of flora, like the *huang-ch'a*, a large leguminous herb whose roots were valued as a remedy against sunstroke.

9

THE END OF THEIR TETHER

They stayed one week in Saratsi to gather their strength before setting off again. David had decided to explore the mountainous region around Wu-t'ang-chiao. They set off on 24 July 1866, a motley crew consisting of David, Sambdatchiemda, Chévrier, and the faithful camel. It was early morning and already 122°F (40°C). They were attired in a mixture of Chinese, Mongolian and European dress. To protect his head from the sun Brother Chévrier wore an old hat of agave pith, a souvenir of the Anglo-French expedition in China. David preferred the Chinese summer hat, the *liang-mao*, cool and shaped like a mushroom draped with thin cloth, but lacking the customary tuft of red yak hair. One great advantage of the *liang-mao* was that it did not squeeze the head, being separated from it by thin strips of bamboo which permitted the air to circulate and perspiration to evaporate as it formed. His butterfly net served as a walking cane, and his gun hung from his shoulder. He had long since come to realise that just to carry arms was sufficient to prevent one from having to use them.

They travelled first among low carboniferous hills, which later yielded to mountains of granite. Clematis with stiff stems and fragrant yellow flowers with light violet anthers were flowering in abundance. David noted the tree sparrow, the rock sparrow, the lark, the grey *Saxicola*, and, more particularly, the falcon. Willows and poplars unerringly signified the presence of dwellings. Every now and then the valleys would echo to the abruptly terminated yell with which Sambdatchiemda, blackened by the summer sun, coaxed the laden camel up the steeper slopes.

By evening they had reached a stream which meandered down towards Saratsi, where several carters were already camped. These carried their own water and dung for fuel and so could stop anywhere they chose on their route. In the summer they slept under their carts, which were just bare planks on rough, wooden wheels. This was as good – and safe – a place as any to camp.

The camel was also tired: it knelt down and then roared to be divested of its load. They ate their millet by the light of the moon. Several falling stars hurtled across the immense sky.

The night was broken by the loud shouts of Chinese shepherds hoping to frighten away the wolves from their sheep and cows, which were fat at this time of the year, and which spent the nights under the stars. But David knew it was pointless to ask the Chinese for milk since they never milk their cows.

The following day they witnessed Chinese 'imperialism' in action. They encountered Chinese farmers in this exclusively Mongol country, armed with mattocks and spades and getting ready to build stone houses. They had just arrived and were living temporarily in tents, near which a fine herd of cattle was grazing. These farmers had chosen for their home the best spot in the area, near a well. They stated that the land belonged to Ming-an and that they had the right to settle there. A little farther along some Mongols maintained exactly the opposite, stating that the country belonged to them, that the Chinese were seizing it unjustly and that the matter had already been brought before the court of justice, but that they feared that the money and deceit of the Chinese would cause an unfair decision in favour of the latter. In that case they would drive the invaders out by force. The Chinese, on their part, fired off their guns from time to time to show the Mongols that they too were armed and were not going to yield. Bloody conflicts of this kind were frequent in the parts of Mongolia invaded by the Chinese; but no matter what the nomadic shepherds of central Asia did, they were not able to hold back the exuberant Chinese population. The descendants of the redoubtable soldiers of Genghis Khan and Tamerlane were now too scattered, too inept, and too lazy. Their country was being depopulated day by day, either through poverty and illness or because of the great number of lamas, and it was the Chinese who were repeopling the land and absorbing the poor wreckage of the Mongol race.

In the distance were Mongol lands. David wondered how long it would be before they too were appropriated by the Chinese. The Mongols were unedu-cated and had no idea of business. They would sell off pieces of land, their heritage, in exchange for some paltry amount of millet, instead of bartering their sheep, cattle and furs for a commodity which they could grow quite easily themselves if they had half a mind to do so. Because of their lack of education, those Mongols who ventured into China were fleeced on all sides by the smart Chinese. Unauthorised and impromptu customs officers extracted money and levies from them for any number of reasons – repairing roads, building bridges, constructing pagodas, etc.

Along the path the expedition passed human skulls and other human bones. The Mongols did not bury their dead. They would simply leave the

They passed long caravans of camels tied
together in file one behind the other, each
with its headrope tied to the pack-saddle of
the beast in front of it.

corpse wherever a lama had indicated would be the most propitious place for a
happy transmigration of the soul. Crows, eagles, wolves and dogs soon attacked the flesh. David was at a loss as to why there were relatively few vultures
and other birds of prey in a land where it would be so easy for them to live. He
was also struck by the fact that there were no scavenging animals, such as
jackals, present; in fact, in all his travels in China David never once came
across a jackal.

The terrain slowly gave way to sandy, sterile country. The mountains
were so denuded and despoiled of shrubs that the travellers had difficulty in
gathering enough twigs and dry herbs to heat their water. Water, too, was
becoming increasingly scarce. They passed long caravans of camels, twelve at a
time tied together in file behind each other, each with its headrope tied to the
pack-saddle of the beast in front of it. Each group of twelve animals was under
one camel-driver. The caravans were taking merchandise from Kweisui to I-li
(now Suiting), in Sinkiang, in central Mongolia. Because water was so scarce
several camels were employed just to carry water.

Mounted lamas would gallop all day long
from one tent to another to kill time.

On the way several lamas passed them. These were a constant source of annoyance, not only to them but also to the poor Mongol population. During the good season well-dressed and mounted lamas would gallop all day long from one tent to another to kill time, sure of being welcomed by the Mongols, though the family provisions would suffer noticeably as a result of their visits. Tea with milk and salt, vinegar and brandy were the delicacies offered to the visitors, and if the family was having a meal when they arrived, politeness demanded that they be invited. That was why the Mongols, who were understandably as miserly as they were poor, generally ate only at night, when they were no longer afraid of receiving visitors.

They camped for the night near some Mongol tents, but they could not sleep because of the large dogs which barked incessantly outside their tent. These dogs were mongrels, and were characterised by their black colour and a reddish-brown spot under each eye and at the base of the paw.

Unexpected and unusually heavy rain delayed their start next day. The sound of tinkling bells, so like the bells used on the cows in his native Pyrenees, attracted David's attention. He peeped out of the tent, and was surprised to see a yak. Yaks – grunting oxen as David called them – had been imported into the region from Tibet about thirty years previously. He smiled as he watched a yak in play, twisting and turning about its tail, which terminated in a broad tuft like a plume of feathers. In his diary David described the yaks in detail.

> This morning I came across a dozen that I am able to examine at my ease. The bull is superb. His horns, very arched, are highly developed, placed on the side instead of the front of his head; his thick hair reaches almost to the ground; his short tail is very furry all the way up. The animal seems to disappear amid the immense mass of wool; however, its movements are brisk. At this season the cows have fairly short hair except on the tail, at the neck, and on the withers. All these animals are entirely black, which is said to be the natural colour of the species. They grunt continually like pigs and graze at their ease on the mountains, which they prefer to the plain, and where they run and jump agilely in places ordinary cattle would avoid. In the evening, at a given signal, they come docilely together around their stable.

Sambdatchiemda recounted to David and Chévrier a remarkable sight he had seen while escorting Fathers Gabet and Huc on their journey to Lhasa. A herd of about fifty yaks had attempted to ford a river at the very instant the waters congealed through the cold. The yaks were bound fast, unable to extricate themselves. Their fine heads, surmounted with great horns, were still

A yak, with its arched horns and thick hair reaching
almost to the ground. The animal seems
to disappear amid an immense mass of wool.

above the surface; their bodies were enclosed by ice which was so transparent, you could see their limbs as if they were still swimming. The eagles and crows had pecked out their eyes. Sambdatchiemda also mentioned that west of Tsinghai there was a species of large wild ox with black hair and enormous horns that frequented the deforested summits of the mountains. Sambdatch-iemda stated that the legendary unicorn also came from those parts. He claimed that he had actually seen a unicorn, admittedly not a live one, but one that had been stuffed and preserved in the large lamasery of Kumbum near Hsi-ning Fu. The size and gait of the unicorn were like those of an antelope, but it differed from the antelope in having one single horn in the centre of its forehead.

Next day they witnessed one of the many calamities that constantly befell the fatalistic people of these regions, who would suddenly see all their worldly wealth, little as it was, and their means of livelihood, vanish before their eyes. Strewn around them were the carcasses of oxen that had succumbed to the epizootic scourge which had made such cruel inroads on the herds some months earlier. In addition, at every step appeared the bones of sheep and goats that had died more recently. A month and a half earlier these animals, especially the goats, had sickened suddenly, spewed a little water from their mouths, and died almost at once. Three-quarters of the herds had evidently died from the disease that year; so the Mongols were poorer than ever.

The large wild ox with enormous horns and
long black hair that frequented the summits
of mountains.

However, the happy-go-lucky people seemed to be little affected by misfortune, to which they were only too well accustomed. Their attitude was exemplified by a bon-vivant lama the travellers met further on, whose total wealth consisted of a few cows and who passed the time playing his flute in his tent.

They reached a place that Sambdatchiemda recognised. He had lived there for two years as a lama about thirty years previously. It was here that a local Mongol who had no children of his own had wanted to adopt Tchy-Lama so that he could inherit his tent and animals. This must have been a great temptation for Sambdatchiemda, then a young man of twenty and with no means, but Sambdatchiemda had resisted the temptation and continued to wear the violet robe of a lama. Imagine the delight when after dinner that evening a visitor arrived who was none other than a former acquaintance of Sambdatchiemda, now an old man of seventy.

In the early hours of the morning Sambdatchiemda staggered into the tent, having left his friend and wife dead drunk. Such behaviour was not considered unbecoming or shameful in Mongolia.

A feminine voice called from the flap of the tent. She was a young girl with black eyes set wide apart but almost hidden (Chinese fashion) under her large lids. She had come on behalf of her parents to offer them a cup of cream and a little pitcher of butter-milk, the favourite drink of the shepherds. Such kindness made David's day.

Shortly after this they had another visitor, a poor eleven-year-old boy from Ordos. His father had been killed in battle, and he was working as a slave in a Mongolian family.

One afernoon while they were passing through a town which had been appropriated by the Chinese, they almost precipitated a riot. As

The legendary unicorn which Sambdatchiemda claimed that he had seen, albeit stuffed, in the lamasery of Kumbum.

was customary in almost all Chinese market-towns or villages, there was a theatre opposite the pagoda. A play was in progress; they approached as unobtrusively as possible. The theatre was built according to the usual model with space only for the actors and a few musicians; the spectators were ranged round the stage on the ground. The instrumental music which accompanied the loud cries and exaggerated gestures of the actors was completely without harmony or chords. One man was playing a flute without keys, a sort of primitive little reed; another was struggling with a large trumpet with an enormous bell on which he could only manage two notes – base and fifth; a third sawed away vigorously on a violin with a small sounding box having two strings to which a bridge was attached; two others made less disagreeable sounds on their guitars. The old fellow who should have been manipulating the eight bells with their false notes had obviously spent his skills on millet brandy, which was the favourite alcoholic drink.

Chinese women obviously enjoyed the theatre. They were there in their brilliantly coloured red, green and violet dresses with wide sleeves reaching to their knees. Their trousers, very wide of the hips, tapered to the ankle, leaving exposed their tiny stunted feet. Their shining black hair was immaculately combed and bedecked with artificial flowers. Mongol women were there too, recognisable in their long dresses, their heads covered with the little round hats peculiar to Mongolia, their hair divided into many braids lifted at the sides of the head. The Chinese men had not gone to the same trouble with their dress; they wore white stockings and perhaps a cleaner vest than usual. The little boys were naked, or almost so, as was the custom in summer.

One of the urchins in the crowd turned round and jumped up in astonishment at the strange dress and wild appearance of David and his band. The other urchins followed suit; soon the entire audience was watching them rather than the play. The man with the feminine face who was playing the role of the heroine was chagrined at losing his audience's attention: he screamed out something. But the audience was far more fascinated at seeing the strange white men for the first time. Many of them began laughing at David and Chévrier. The two missionaries laughed back, pleased at having provided a free spectacle for the people. Before the

Spectators clustered around the raised stage of a local theatre.

performance degenerated into utter chaos they passed as quickly as possible through the village, pursued none the less by a jolly crowd.

The next day, 5 August, was marked by misfortune.

'Sambdatchiemda! What's the matter?' David asked anxiously of Tchy-Lama, who was in obvious distress. It was a recurrence of the dysentery which he had failed to shake off completely and which had finally weakened him so that he could barely stand. His propensity for *chao-chiu*, the strong and vile-smelling Chinese brandy, to which he would add cloves of garlic to heat his throat, as was the Mongol custom, had further aggravated his health.

'Oh! No!' It was a groan from Chévrier.

'What's the matter?' David inquired.

'Look!' David looked at the camel. It stood there, a most pathetic figure, its stomach mightily distended, due, no doubt, to consuming vast quantities of pigweed.

Without the camel their progress would be extremely slow; without their guide, Sambdatchiemda, they would be lost. David plied Sambdatchiemda with some medicaments from his first-aid box. But he had no medicaments for the camel. Sambdatchiemda, too, realised their predicament. After some time he went out of the tent into the brush and then returned. He made for the camel, and forced a long steel awl deeply into five points in the belly of the animal. The Mongols believed that if blood was drawn by this operation the animal would be saved; if not, it would die. Sambdatchiemda held up the long needle: blood was visible on it.

Amazingly, the camel improved during the course of the day and was quite cured the next day. But not Tchy-Lama. Reluctantly David accepted that he would have to change his plans. He had hoped to visit the country of the Ordos, where the remains of the great Genghis Khan were reputedly carefully preserved, enclosed in a large silver casket which the Mongols did not readily permit strangers to see. Pilgrims from far and wide went there and made their prostrations, after kissing the casket, which was wrapped in precious mate-rials. The focus of this pilgrimage was about 100 miles (160 km) south-west of Saratsi, in a place called Ttia-y-seng. With luck he might even have found the elusive blue pheasant there. But such a journey was not now possible: the immediate concern was to return to Saratsi and restore Sambdatchiemda to health. David could still put his

A theatre performance in action.

time to effective use. His herbarium was considerable and contained many new specimens, but the difficulties of being constantly on the move, aggravated by the vagaries of the weather and lack of sufficient preserving paper, meant that his specimens had not been prepared as carefully as he would have liked. He would use the stay in Saratsi to repair any damage to his specimens and to complete the descriptive notes which must accompany each specimen – in a word, do everything possible to ensure that the fruits of his labours would not be lost to science.

The steep mountain overlooking Saratsi, which David had earlier tried to scale unsuccessfully, came into view. Maybe he would try once more; he was not one who took defeat lightly.

Leaving Sambdatchiemda in Brother Chévrier's capable hands, David set off the next day, to tackle the mountain again, even though the lamas had told him that only kites and eagles could reach the summit, since the razor-like ravines and fissures defied any access to it. The west side of the peak looked promising for plants: he would attempt that route.

Slowly but sure-footedly he got higher and higher up the mountain. From rock to rock he picked his way towards a large fissure thick with shrubbery, and from here he was finally able to haul himself triumphantly to the summit. An enormous bearded vulture with a pale yellow abdomen approached alarmingly close to investigate this uninvited intruder who had invaded its sanctuary. Stretching far below and to the horizon were the plains, some green, some yellow, of the Ordos, traversed by the majestic sweeps of the great Hoang-Ho. David's diary records the next harrowing hour.

> I do not remain long on this dangerous peak. The view is really beautiful, but my eyes glaze over and my heart quivers at the sight of the frightening precipices several hundred metres high which surround me, and from which I must make my descent. So I leave the narrow peak and crawl carefully along the fissure which led me there, holding on to the Thuya, Ephedra bearing sweet red berries, Phyllanthus, etc., which abound in it. Finally I arrive in a safe place, a little grotto, where I thank God for having prevented me from breaking my neck. I tremble when I see the abyss into which the slightest distraction might have precipitated me. Everyone knows that in this kind of climbing the difficult part is not going up, but coming down; it is especially then that one sees the open abysses under one's feet, and that one can easily lose the coolness and equilibrium which are essential. Fortunately I was alone. There is nothing

more dangerous than to have witnesses to the risks one has to undergo. Their fear is always greater than yours and compounds your own hesitation. I was not rewarded for my exhausting ascent by much enrichment of my botanical and insect collections.

On re-entering Saratsi the desperate straits of the people became evident. Drought had played havoc with the crops. By now their own provisions had also almost run out, but the excessive heat and dryness continued. They found all the shops closed. The city fathers had imposed eight days of strict prayer and penance and fasting for rain. Merchants were forbidden to sell any food. The drought continued despite the prayers and lamentations of the lamas and of the people. Tom-toms and tambourines beat out a steady rhythm from morning to night in pagodas, where only widows, young girls and little children, considered to be without sin, were allowed to offer prayers. Men, all considered to be sinners, were forbidden entry to the pagodas. Instead they carried statues of Lung-wang, the god of rain, from shrines to streams, in supplication for rain. A special invocation was even made to the great Hoang-Ho, but all to no avail. One shrewd lama was going round the streets guaranteeing he could make it rain in three days, on the condition that he was paid in advance. But even the gullible Mongols did not fall for that.

Both David and Chévrier jumped as three cannon shots shook the apartment. 'What was that?' wondered the startled Chévrier.

'Oh, that's nothing,' Sambdatchiemda casually volunteered. 'It's to announce the opening of the theatre in a nearby village.' David went back to his taxidermy.

'Where are you going?' Chévrier asked. David turned to see Tchy-Lama preparing to leave.

'That village,' Sambdatchiemda replied, 'for food.'

By now Sambdatchiemda had begun to regain his former health. He explained that Chinese fasts were not held simultaneously in different towns and villages, so he could buy some provisions there.

'But you know what the penalty is if they catch you breaking the fast.' The huge shoulders shrugged as the fearless Dchiahour stepped out into the road.

That evening they were able to disregard, though covertly, the strict imposition of penance and fasting. It was 15 August, the feast of the Assumption. They celebrated with coffee and some French cognac which the worthy brother had secreted away in his leather bag, saving it for a grand occasion. The same evening David was able to give some sympathy and friendship to a poor wretch dying in the cabin next to theirs, emaciated from opium, but who nevertheless had just about enough strength to ask again for the drug that was killing him.

The next day it was David's turn to succumb to the months of fatigue and privation. His rheumatic pains were much worse; and he had a high fever to boot. The days went by. As Sambdatchiemda and the camel regained their strength, David became progressively worse. Reluctantly he had to abandon his plans for further exploration. The heat in the sandy plains of the Ordos would be unendurable in his condition, and there would be the ever-present aggravations of the Tartar soldiers to contend with. He would be advancing, moreover, into rebel territory. As the final straw, local travellers had stated quite categorically that it would be impossible to get the camel across the Hoang-Ho. David began to make plans for the return to Peking.

And then, suddenly, the rains came. Saratsi changed form a dead or dying town to one where fire-crackers and music and gaiety announced a festival of thanksgiving.

They managed to hire two carts for their enormous amount of baggage – the tent, sleeping bags, provisions, cooking utensils, changes of clothes, herbarium specimens, boxes containing zoological specimens, samples of rocks, all squeezed into any vacant space. On 27 August they set off on foot from Saratsi, the carts piled high, on the first leg of their journey back to Peking, the 120-mile (195 km) trip to Kweisui. They met other carts, filled with women and girls, all dressed in their most brilliantly coloured finery – red, blue and green – on their way to the celebrations in thanksgiving for the rains. The three travellers had not shaved in weeks; long beards covered their tanned faces, wizened from constant fatigue and hunger. They presented a wild, down-and-out appearance, in contrast to the cavalcades of lamas that passed them, dressed in their finest saffron and crimson robes, who laughed with disdain at David and his party.

Loud shouting brought David and his party to a halt. A man galloped up. More trouble, thought David. But no, it was Thao-tchy, the 'Mongol-Chinese', grinning from ear to ear, wanting to wish the party well. That made up for the rude hostility David had had to endure during their sojourn in Saratsi. Thao-tchy was a soldier who had fought against Europeans and come to respect them the more. David had noticed the same respect from other Mongol soldiers who had been defeated by the Europeans in the 1860s.

They travelled slowly. This time there were going to be no short-cuts or deviations to explore virgin territory. They kept to the main highway, and joined other travellers whenever possible to have some security in numbers against the ever-present bandits and Hui-hui.

As they journeyed the country became more picturesque; the fields were more fertile and trees more numerous. *Mows* (acre plots) of wheat swayed in the wind; fields of melons and watermelons abounded near the villages. Plots of *pai-ts'ai* (Chinese cabbage), broad beans, peas, turnips, radishes and spinach added variety to the fields of vegetables in flower. A quartet of quails flapped over the millet fields.

They reached the old city of Kweisui at noon on 30 August. Sentries were pacing the ramparts of the high crenellated walls. A crowd of threatening spectators closed in on the travellers, and a fat well-dressed lama, a revolting specimen, supported by other equally revolting characters, accosted them. Only when David promised they would not be stopping in the city were they allowed to go on.

They travelled on to Erh-shih-san-hao, a journey of seven days, on foot. They had hoped to hire some ponies or donkeys to ride at Kweisui but their rude expulsion had denied them even a chance to rest. By now David was stopping with increasing frequency, feeling very ill with his high fever and dysentery. Chévrier and Sambdatchiemda were both concerned, but David would not heed their entreaties to offload some of his collections and take their place in one of the carts. He collapsed several times on the way and was in a dead faint for some time.

In the heat of the day they rested while they could, and marched in the evenings and at dusk. The first white frosts heralded the onset of the cold season. Again on arrival at Erh-shih-san-hao David collapsed, exhausted by fatigue and fever. The party rested some days before setting off again. At Kalgan Brother Chévrier left them to return to his mission. He knew David

Sentries on guard walked on the ramparts of the high crenellated walls guarding the city.

was in the good hands of Tchy-Lama and it was not too far to Suanhwa. At Suanhwa David met his Chinese helper, Ouang Thomè, who had looked after the collections of plants and animals. It was a sad day, however, for David and Sambdatchiemda as they parted, David for Peking and Tchy-Lama for his native village. The two men, who had shared so many dangers together, who would each have given his life for the other, who had suffered enormous hardships and privations together, and who, quite often, had got on each other's nerves, clasped each other tightly.

On 26 October, after an absence of seven and a half months, David finally arrived back in Peking. He had covered a distance, often on foot, of some 1,000 miles (1,600 km) to Mongolia and back. He had endured terrible hardships of travel under the most primitive and rigorous of conditions, withstanding the sandstorms of the Mongolian steppes, and the withering barrenness of the Gobi Desert, enduring lack of food and water for long periods, fighting off wild, marauding bandits, suffering persecution and succumbing to severe illness.

It was as a result of this journey that the western world first received any complete knowledge of the plants and animals of the then largely unexplored and unknown region now known as Inner Mongolia. David returned with the skins of 150 birds and mammals. His herbarium consisted of 124 species of plants; his insect collection contained over 260 species.

David enjoyed being back with his fellow priests at the College in Peking, and they were curious to hear of his many adventures. The blue pheasant had eluded him, but as far as he could ascertain the unicorn really did exist: his faithful guide Sambdatchiemda had seen a stuffed one at a lamasery in Kumbum. The celebrated explorer Huc, a Vincentian priest like David, mentions that many villages in Tibet derived their names from the unicorns which lived in their midst; for example, the village of Serin-Dziong, which means village of the land of the unicorns, situated near the Chinese border.

What about the *pei-hsuing*, which means white bear in Chinese? No, he had not seen one, but a chronicle of AD 621 refers to a 'white bear with black spots' inhabiting the bamboo forests in the mountains near Tibet. Maybe, just as the supposedly legendary unicorn did once exist, the white bear with black spots also once existed.

No, he had not encountered a Chinese dragon, nor the 'missing link'! David did not mind having his leg pulled.

Chinese soldiers.

10

THE SECOND JOURNEY
OF EXPLORATION

Père David was not satisfied with what he had achieved. 'The collections I made and sent to France were not brilliant, for the high Mongol plateaux are desperately poor in every respect.' He concedes that 'nevertheless a number of animal and plant species, some new to science and others of interest to zoogeography were secured'. By now David had made a remarkable number of discoveries. Apart from *Elaphurus davidianus* (Père David's deer), there was *Dipus annulatus* (a gerbil), which he found in the plains of Mongolia; *Siphneus armandii*, found on the Mongolian high plateau; *Rhizomys vestitus*, found near Lake Koko Nor; *Arvicola mandarinus*, found in Chinese Mongolia, the antelope Candata, *Meles leucoloemys*, and *Sciurius davidianus*, all discovered in the north-west region of Peking. Among the flowers were *Davidia involucrata, Buddleia davidii, Lilium davidii, Viburnum davidiana, Prunus davidiana, Stranvaesia davidiana, Clematis davidiana, Clematis armandii, Adonis davidii, Astilbe chinensis davidii*. These were the names later given to these flowers by the French Academy of Sciences in Paris.

Among the many birds he had discovered was *Pterorhinus davidi* and *Syrnium davidi*, and others of different shapes, sizes and colours. And there were butterflies too. His fish specimens, however, had been a disappointment: the Chinese alcohol Père David had used had not proved effective. He would do better next time!

By now David had come to realise that perhaps he could be of more service to the Church by devoting his life to scientific research than by trying to convert the Chinese. He began planning another journey of exploration. This time he intended to go up the Blue River (the Yangtze), across the large province of Szechwan, and then to the independent principalities of eastern Tibet.

Prior to setting off David made the usual round of courtesy calls to the legations of France, England, Russia, Spain and the United States. From Dr

Martin of the French Legation he was able to get medicaments to overcome the fever and dysentery which had plagued him on his earlier expedition.

At the British Legation David felt undressed in the midst of so many medals, sashes and decorations. He had received no medals for facing the bloodthirsty bandits of Tartary or for just ministering to the sick and the poor. Sir Rutherford Alcock received him hospitably, and they got into a friendly discussion. David was sorry to learn that Mr Robert Swinhoe, the famous ornithologist and English Consul, had been held up and would not be in Peking for another week. It was a pity as David had been looking forward to meeting him.

'Risking your neck for plants and animals! You must be . . .' The minister plenipotentiary stopped in time. David smiled.

'Yes, my friends think I'm crazy too!'

Lady Alcock had so much wanted to meet David. She had *such* a surprise for him . . . a tortoise with green hairs growing out of its shell! She led David to her room, where this unusually rare reptile was housed. It certainly was remarkable, David thought, as he carefully examined the somnolent, docile animal. He smiled to himself. Should he tell her or not? He decided not to: she would be so disappointed. The supposed hairs were long aquatic marine plants that had been parasitically established on the hard shell of the amphibious reptile. That night David wrote in his diary: 'The Chinese are the cleverest frauds in the world.'

Sir Rutherford appraised David of the latest political situation: the brigands, the Taipans, in the central provinces, had joined up with the rebel Muslims from Kansu and had already invaded the provinces of Shantung and Pei-chi-li, pillaging, killing, massacring, and looting on the way. The imperial troops, badly organised, poorly paid and undernourished, refused to march against the rebel hordes. Those that did fight were cut to pieces, leaving behind valuable English and American weapons for the rebels. The remainder of the imperial troops were said to be in league with the plunderers. They had probably already taken over the territory around Tientsin, and were planning to move into Peking. The imperial T'ung Chih family had made plans to flee into Tartary if that happened.

The rebel Muslims were descended from the ancient migrations from Turkestan, and were a violent and bloodthirsty people. Everything in the towns they inhabited bore the marks of violence. No one of them walked the streets without a huge sabre at his side, which was used at the slightest provocation. Not an hour passed without some violent street combat. They were a prosperous and powerful people, and even had a mosque in Lhasa, where the people would stand aside to let them pass.

David passed through an outer gate in the
great wall of Peking, topped by a massive fort,
to start his second journey of exploration,
which took him nearly 3,000 miles (5,000 km)
and lasted two years, during which he made
stunning plant and animal discoveries, but
which left him virtually dead from illness.

The diary entry for 25 May 1868, reads: 'Tomorrow I begin an expedition which will take three years and which will take me far from Peking yet I feel as serene as if it were a question of a short walk.'

Some short walk! His exploration was to cover a distance of several thousand miles, not counting the side excursions.

David left Peking the following day, three carters dragging an enormous

One variety of vehicle, like a wheelbarrow,
used for transporting goods.

covered wagon, more like a wheelbarrow, which carried his goods and baggage. He regretted that this time, despite all Sambdatchiemda's surliness and temperamental behaviour, he was not there to accompany him. He would miss his company, especially if he met with the cut-throat rebels. He was glad, however, to be leaving this city of immense human anthills, bustling with frenetic energy. There were people everywhere: on foot, on carts, on animals, a million feet and wheels raising the choking dust. The women stood and stared as his strange cavalcade passed: some in short blue cotton pants, with small feet and unkempt hair, their babies on hip; others in blouses and skirts, or trousers and tunics. Some carried coloured paper parasols.

The party slowly made its way to the outer gate, moving out of the way as camels waltzed and floundered on the broken flagstones. A little string of donkeys easily overtook them; they in turn managed to squeeze past a cart laden with sacks of millet drawn lazily by a team of five oxen. David stopped to watch a black bear being led on a chain. The traffic became less congested once they had passed out of the city gates. A pony marched behind a troop of camels, her nose under the tail of the last camel.

Soon David was in the open country. Winnowers threw up a series of golden jets which fanned out into fine golden clouds. A naked boy astride a huge buffalo, up to its knees in a paddy-field, waved his straw hat. They made a detour to avoid the great salt marsh east of Peking.

By noon David had reached Tunghsien. The crowds got more and more dense; there were people everywhere.

'Father David! Father David!' It was the voice of Ouang Thomè, the young Pekinese helper who had accompanied David on his first journey to Mongolia. Despite his ability to fall asleep at the most unfortunate times, Ouang had the eyes of a lynx. David had arranged specially to have him accompany him as a hunter. They walked along a road called the street of 'Everlasting Prosperity'. David could not understand why. Eventually they reached the junction of the Pei-Ho and the Yu-Ho or Grand Canal. The waterway was covered with flat-bottomed barges. Thomè had managed to rent

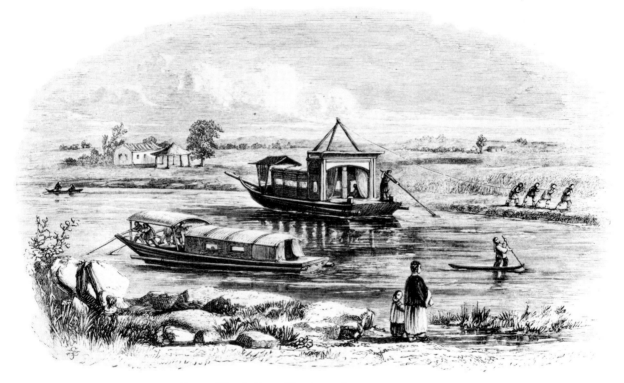

Covered flat-bottomed boats, used
extensively on the rivers in China.

a covered boat for the short journey to Tientsin, but only after a great deal of trouble. No less than 20,000 candidates had descended on the capital to compete for their doctorate degrees and were now returning home after their examinations.

The Pei-Ho was as calm and smooth as a mirror as the two boatmen, one in front and one in the rear, propelled the boat through the salt, muddy water. David anxiously eyed his baggage, perched high and precariously in the middle of the boat, as it shuddered in the wash of a large houseboat being hauled by ropes by a team of men on the bank. Sandpipers darted here and there, uttering their timid, faint cries. Occasionally they passed a black drongo, its plumes reflecting all the colours of a drop of oil on water, a few long feathers without barbules flowing like a mane from its head. The villagers respected the drongo, not only because they ate many insects, but because they were also endowed with great courage and would fight off crows and kites, the usual scavengers of the poultry yard. Apart from a few willows growing in the villages, the vegetation along the shores of the river was minimal, not even a few shrubs.

In the evening the boat stopped, for the simple reason that the Chinese do not travel at night. Occasional flashes of sheet lightning lit up the distant sky.

The next morning, David was troubled to see a corpse floating down the river. This was not a particularly rare sight: people were often too poor to afford coffins and so the relatives would consign the bodies to the river. This year the poverty had been aggravated by the severe drought. Many people were reduced to eating wild herbs, roots, leaves and even the bark of trees. Often, too, the river carried the savagely and indecently mutilated corpses of those who had met their fate at the hands of the marauding brigands. There were no vultures to hasten the dissolution of the corrupting masses. Only large flights of wild fowl on their southerly migration from the plains of Manchuria made for the low reeds and tangle of the salt pools, ditches, rush-girt marshes and quaking bogs.

Increasing traffic on the river heralded the approach to the rich commercial city of Tientsin. Large fields of tall waving millet (*sorghum*), from which the local brandy was made, and maize lined the banks. Eventually, beyond the huge grassy plain they could pick out the long crenellated mud walls which encircled the city. It was five o'clock in the evening when they finally neared it. Each bank of the river was defended by a wall of earthen redoubts armed with cannon and manned here and there with pockets of Chinese soldiers. Hedges of pointed bamboo stakes in the ground in front of the redoubts guarded their approaches. The little boat literally had to fight its way through a veritable wall of war-boats which spanned the river to keep away the rebels who were reputedly within a few miles of the city. David was agreeably

The French Residency in Tientsin.

surprised to see the tricolour flying from the masts of two French gunboats –
the *Aspic* and the *Lebrethon*. The presence of these men-of-war provided some
reassurance to the frightened population: the *Ch'ang-mao* (the long-haired
rebels) would be received with cannon shot if they encroached too near the city
of Tientsin.

The French Legation was built in Chinese pagoda style. An armed
legionnaire, with a long musket over his shoulder, peered out from an open
square cupola, adorned with a pagoda roof in the shape of a bell. The boat
pulled alongside the wooden building which served as David's Order's mission
house. Father Tchoung, a Chinese priest, was there to welcome David and
Thomè. In the distant past the emperor used to stay here at the mission house
while travelling from his northern court in Peking to the southern court in
Nanking. The locals still resented seeing 'western devils' in a residence of the
'Son of Heaven'.

David heard with pleasure of the sterling work being done by the handful
of missionaries at Tientsin. Each year about 20,000 adults were baptised, after
a very exhausting probation and instruction lasting one year for each catechu-

men. What was hindering their work of evangelisation was the example of the other Europeans in the city, who were far from being models of piety and virtue; though they did not frequent the opium dens as much as the Chinese did themselves, they were certainly no strangers to the many brothels that were to be found in the city. This was what the Chinese reported to the Fathers at the mission.

David set off for the street that housed the wealthy merchants who monopolised the North China junk trade. The men were well dressed in their long blue frocks. Carved pillars decorated some of the business premises. The Fathers at the mission had booked him a passage on a junk that was to leave in a day or two for Shanghai. David wanted to check that everything was in order. Yes, as he expected: everything was in order, and the junk would sail in good Chinese time – two weeks later!

Excitement was high in the city. The *Ch'ang-mao* were believed to be only a few miles away and an attack by their leader, Yen-wang (King of Hell) was expected anytime. Amidst all the panic, with refugees scurrying out of the city with their little bundles of belongings on their heads, or in carts, if they had them, David was intrigued by a mandarin, completely unperturbed, hunting hares with a falcon. He had already caught nearly three dozen.

That evening David met a young French officer at the mission. He was Captain Lebarrière, in command of the *Lebrethon*. He was horrified to learn that David had planned to cover the 1,000 miles (1,600 km) of the Yellow Sea to Shanghai by junk: the China coast was crawling with pirate boats. The authorities had no control over these pirates, who took a regular toll of junks and similar unarmed boats, like wolves harrying a flock of sheep. The *Lebrethon, en route* to Shanghai, was in dock having one of its engines repaired, and the captain would be happy to give David a lift. David was delighted.

David decided to see for himself the good work of the Sisters of Charity that he had heard so much about. They had only been in existence for six years but their work in education and medicine, their devotion and their virtues had won the esteem of the entire population, Christian and pagan.

He crossed over the Pei-Ho river by means of the floating bridge composed of logs and planking laid on top of boats. The harbour was encumbered with imperial boats bringing rice to the Emperor from the south. There were junks under sail, laden with sacks of salt; sampans, with their bamboo hatches, bobbed up and down everywhere in the water. He passed the sampan jetty and then the fish market with its rows of pallid mullet carefully laid out; the hawkers shouted their wares. The market stalls were pink with the juicy pulp of watermelons, speckled and blackened with the plague of flies that buzzed everywhere. Hands gesticulated wildly amidst a babel of dialects. The smell of

A wealthy merchant. Carved pillars decorate his business premises.

fresh fruit and vegetables – apples, peaches, pears, apricots, grapes, pumpkins, cabbages, onions, garlic – vied with the stink of salted fish and preserved vegetables. Men with empty baskets and strings of copper cash thrown casually over their shoulders made their way home, or to the opium dens. The anxious screech of the fillet sweep could just be heard over the general din and hubbub. Little flycatchers darted into the air to catch the passing flies. Warblers, buntings, sparrows, goldcrests and yellow cranes flew from one spot to another through the heat haze. Hawkers selling ice scuttled around everywhere. During the heat of the day the Chinese would lie on mats on top of crushed ice scattered over the stove-couch. It was now well into the Chinese summer. The scorching winds that swept across the open plain around Tientsin added their store of discomfort. David was glad to rest in the shade of the Haikwang (Glory of the Queen) Monastery. He did not have far to walk now. He passed the two-storeyed pagoda, in the courtyard of which flourished a few bier-trees. Unripe fruit, which the Europeans called Shanghai dates, hung from their branches. The upper floor of the pagoda was full of large ugly josses.

He finally reached the House of the Sisters, and passed under the trellised vines which formed a leafy bower. Of the ten Sisters at the House six were French, two Belgian, one English and one Italian. There were also several young Chinese girls who were postulants for the Order.

When he got back to the mission David expressed his concern about the Sisters. They lived in the very heart of the city and were entirely at the mercy of the Chinese. What a field day the rebels – and the following rabble – would have if they decided to attack.

In the early hours of the morning of 6 June 1868, the *Lebrethon*, its repairs completed, slipped from its dock at Su-t'chu-lin and made its way down the sinuous river. The rain pelted down. On more than one occasion the gunboat ran aground on the numerous shoals. The sirens hooted as they passed other European steamboats and sailing ships. Two days later they passed Taku, left the river and headed out to sea. The sea, which was calm at first, soon became rough, the gunboat rolling heavily and David paying his compliments to navigation with a violent attack of seasickness.

As they approached the islands of Miao Tao along the coast of Shantung province, the weather improved, and so did David. In the distance the sharp peaks of the mountains rose up from the dunes. Gulls and cormorants and oyster-catchers winged to and from their nests on the islands; some large grey petrels skimmed and twisted over the water. An octopus could be seen in the shallower waters. Numerous swifts with white bellies flew over the lighthouse which stood elegantly on the highest peak of one of the islands.

The waterway at Shanghai. Junks and
houseboats, sampans and sailing ships, vessels
of every size and shape, jammed the river.

The Custom House at Shanghai. Throngs of
people congregated outside the symmetrical
pagoda-like building.

The bay of Yen-t'ai, or Chefoo, was beautiful. Seven European sailing
ships and six steamboats were at anchor. The shores surrounding the bay had a
gentle slope and the land rose gradually to form purple mountains on the
horizon. Chinese boats were fishing for mackerel or swordfish or turbot. On
the banks grew the cultivated groves of oak, the leaves of which were fed to the
silkworms which furnished the famous pongee silk. Here and there flowered
the convolvulus and statice with red flowers.

As the fog cleared in the morning of 12 June the yellow colour of the
water indicated they were approaching the mouth of that massive Chinese
waterway, the Yangtze. That evening the *Lebrethon* entered the Yangtze and
dropped anchor in the river, which was so wide at its mouth one could not see
its banks. The next morning they made their way slowly up the Blue River and
ascended its tributary, the Huang-p'u, on which Shanghai is built. Finally they
reached the city at three o'clock that afternoon. It was raining. David had been
warned that, unlike Peking which enjoyed at least 300 dry days a year, in

Shanghai it rained one day out of three. Junks and houseboats and sampans and sailing ships – vessels of every size and shape – were jammed on the waterway. Many of the junks had large eyes painted on their bows, and indeed the waters were so congested they would certainly need eyes to make any progress. Crowds of people thronged outside the symmetrical, pagoda-like building, which was the Custom House.

David's diary for the day records: 'The sight of this city makes a great impression on me; it is so long since I have been used to grandeur, ease and cleanliness.'

As he was taking in the message of one of the many rice-paper hoardings above the street David was aware of someone jostling up against him. He placed his hand over the pocket containing his few valuables.

'Pst,' a voice whispered.

'No, thank you. I don't want to see a cock fight and I don't smoke the pipe,' David said emphatically as he brushed off his accoster. Pimps and hawkers of every vice imaginable were on the streets of what was quite obviously a wicked city.

At Shanghai Father David met another missionary, Father Jamet, who had just returned from a successful exploration of the Mekong River. Father Jamet told David that going up the Yangtze at that time of year would certainly be dangerous, if not impossible, since the river would be in flood. Moreover, it was not only by drowning that the mighty Yangtze river each year took a huge toll of victims. Even for those who could swim there was the ever-present hazard of the alligators that inhabited the river. Even at the best of times a boat took more than a month to cover the 600 miles (965 km) between Hankow and Chungking, in Szechwan province. Father Jamet also volunteered the information that, while much of Szechwan was now deforested, the high mountains to the west, near Tibet, were still densely wooded and contained many interesting animals. David respected the advice of so experienced a traveller as Father Jamet. He decided to wait till the mighty Yangtze had subsided to its winter level before continuing his journey.

He was told that some of the Europeans of Shanghai were in the habit of keeping strange, exotic caged birds. It was in this way that he first set eyes on the magnificent *Tragopan temmincki*, the Chinese oriole with its glorious yellow plumage, the oriental partridge, the silver pheasant and the mandarin duck with its blue-green head. The last two birds were imported from Japan, where they were bred.

Through the good offices of the Russell Company David was able to get a half fare to Kiukiang as a missionary on one of their steamboats going to Hankow. On the evening of 23 June, one month after he had set off from

The City of Nanking.

Peking, he boarded the *Hirado*. However, since the Chinese did not travel at night, the Hirado did not begin its long journey up the Yangtze until the following morning. All day the ship struggled against the current of the mighty river, whose banks could scarcely be seen. At Chinkiang and Nanking other travellers joined the boat. The small cabins were soon teeming with Chinese and even though David was in a less crowded cabin, he was continually discomfited as gusts of wind blew in his direction the opium the Chinese were leisurely smoking.

The shores got closer and closer as the river narrowed and with that the journey became more interesting. On the banks of the river he could see the crab-eating herons; and cuckoos, rose-coloured starlings and drongos occasionally paid their respects to the *Hirado*. Towards the south mountains could be seen. Were these the ones he would be exploring? Although now far from the sea, two white porpoises showed their backs as they gambolled in the rust-coloured water. A greenish-brown turtle, with green neck and little yellow eyes, slowly meandered out of the ship's path. Several large black butterflies fluttered about the little masthead. Soon the high mountains of

Mokou were clearly visible, their sides draped in plantations from which came the tea so well-known by that name.

A massive tower picturesquely sited on an isolated rock heralded the opening that led into the famous Lake Poyang. Finally they reached Kiukiang, the 'city of nine rivers', formerly an important centre of commerce that supported a large population. Its advantageous position on the mighty river and its proximity to Lake Poyang had made it a large market-place for tea. Here, too, had come the celebrated porcelain from the adjoining province of Kiangsi, but no longer: the war against the Taiping rebels had taken a heavy toll both of the trade and of the population.

Kiukiang was one of the interior ports open to European commerce. Here the Vincentian Fathers, the followers of the humble Saint Vincent de Paul, friend of the poor, who had founded his mission congregation in Paris two and a half centuries before, had established a mission station. It was here that David was to stay for three months, until the floodwaters of the Yangtze made navigation possible.

11

IN AND AROUND KIUKIANG

On the day after his arrival in Kiukiang, the inquisitive David went into the walled city; it was deserted. Only recently it had been pillaged and plundered by the Taiping rebels, an undisciplined horde of brigands and pitiless assassins. The marauders had descended upon the hapless population and cut the throats of so many people that, according to one eye-witness who survived, the corpses filled the whole of one of the lakes. Not only had the rebels massacred whole sections of the population, they had destroyed everything in their path, down to the trees and vegetation. The nearby province of Chiang-nan had been similarly devastated; vast stretches that were once heavily populated were now veritable deserts inhabited only by leopards and other wild animals.

At supper that evening his fellow missionaries regaled him with such hair-raising stories that he found it hard to differentiate between fact and fiction. Father Celso, who, though only thirty-eight, had a snow-white crop of hair, told him of the frog that barked louder than a dog, and of a completely black wolf. Monseigneur Baldus, the apostolic vicar of the province, told him that in a former mission of his in the region west of Honan, some villagers took away the young cubs from a female wolf. The she-wolf sniffed out the house to which they had been taken but was unable to rescue her young. In retaliation, she carried away the puppies of a female dog to a cave, where she raised them as her own.

These dogs were encountered later: they were as savage as true wolves, and even their voices had changed. Then there was the appropriately named *wa-wa-yii* fish that cried. And Monseigneur Baldus could vouch for this: not only had he seen one, but he had actually eaten one! David decided to find out for himself!

He realised that by staying in the city of Kiukiang he would not add much to his natural history collection, and decided to spend his time more purposefully in a disused seminary some miles to the south of the city. Accompanied by his faithful servant Ouang Thomè, he set off for Nazareth, the rather oddly named seminary. The almost constant rain had churned up the roads into morasses. They passed houses built of walls of mud mixed with chopped straw, resting on layers of reeds introduced about 1 foot (30 cm) from the ground between the upper part of the wall and the foundation. The roofs were thatched with rushes and covered with a thick coating of mud, also mixed with bits of straw. The rain dissolved the mud, which streamed in torrents from the roof-tops, turning the streets into gutters of knee-deep mud. The better houses had tiled roofs.

They hired a boat and two boatmen rowed them across Lake Tranquille to Nazareth, situated at the south end of the lake, which was like glass. How aptly named, thought David. Enormous pelicans pecked leisurely at the abundant fish. As they neared the centre of the lake a slight drizzle began; the glass surface became more and more broken as the wind whipped up small wavelets across the water. The waves got bigger. The two boatmen, their faces lowered against the rain, now pelting down, pulled hard on their oars. A flock of grey herons fled from the storm in V-formation; the black and white water-pheasants with gold spots on their throats and long, very narrow, tails, which the Chinese called *shui-chi*, made for the refuge of the shores. Ouang Thomè and David soon found their umbrellas provided no protection at all against the relentless driving wind and rain. They were soon completely drenched. Anxiously David watched as the boat got nearer and nearer to a floating mass of aquatic plants. He had presumed that the boatmen could see them. He shouted a warning; they pulled hard on the oars but to no avail: the strong wind blew the frail boat into the dark green mass of vegetation which then held them fast. The more the oarsmen struggled to get out of the web the more entangled their oars became.

They had no option but to sit out the storm. When it finally abated another boat came to their assistance and extricated them from the heavy, clinging, floating vegetation.

What would have been a twenty-minute walk to Nazareth took them hours. The rain had turned what had been a road into a river of mud. They tried crossing by some paddy-fields, but this proved even worse; as one foot sank into the brown ooze up to the knee it was only with great difficulty that one could extract one's foot without losing a shoe. The stench from the burial mounds was very pronounced as the rain washed away the soil from the shallow graves. There was little vegetation as all the valuable camphor trees had been destroyed by the rebels.

At long last they reached Nazareth, a deserted, tumble-down wooden house, built in European style, in which some of David's Chinese colleagues

110

had studied as young men. The Pied Piper of Hamelin must also have lived here: there were rats and mice and bandicoots everywhere. But David and Ouang soon established their territorial rights.

David spent the days going out from Nazareth, adding to his large collection of plants and animals. Saxifrages, begonias and primulas were plentiful. He found the large camellia tree, from whose fruit the Chinese extracted oil, mainly for lighting. When the rain became too heavy he spent the day indoors, mounting his specimens. He was particularly delighted with his capture of the rare *Cucubus micropterus* Gould, a magnificent bird which Mr Swinhoe, the English Consul-cum-naturalist, had described in his writings on Chinese ornithology.

Passing the days was no problem; but the nights were unbelievably tiresome. If he and Ouang were not attacked by the rats, they were devoured by gnats and mosquitoes. He had not been troubled with these insects in Kiukiang; there the fish in the lakes destroyed them and their larvae. But here, in the midst of the shallow waters in the rice-fields and mud-flats there were no fish to kill these pests. And despite the presence of their Homeric enemies, the rats, the frogs, too, boldly established themselves in the building. Their constant croaking was something to be heard! It was a welcome change to hear the melodious song of the coot. Occasionally he was able to pick out the croak of the tree-frog, which he had not met before in China.

David was also keen to see the famous Lake Poyang, which was so large that it took a boat eight to ten days to cross, so he and Ouang set off to do that. They aimed at first for Ly Shan: from a high mountain there a view of the lake was possible. On the way they saw and collected several useful plants and animals and David watched carefully for a unique species of porcupine that was said to inhabit the mountains. Now and again they crossed the tracks of wolves.

The look of joy in Ouang's face was infectious. They were both tired and hungry, and a pheasant had landed just near them. What a meal! thought Ouang. But David did not reach for his gun. As he wrote:

> I observe the principle of never killing an animal not needed for my natural history collections. I find it less distressing to feed myself with only rice or millet than to kill one of these poor creatures, who revel in life so joyously and do not harm nature, but on the contrary embellish it. This attitude is not always agreeable to my servants, especially when it is a question of pheasants, but I hold firmly to my rule.

The pagoda stood out, elegant and distinct against the skyline, pointing dramatically like some obelisk into the sky. Its storeys, each diminishing in size as the building soared upwards, were a monument to Chinese architectural skill. At the foot of the pagoda dwellings were visible: so they could perhaps procure shelter for the night. They made their way up the winding road, through groves of elms and wild fig trees. The land around any pagoda is always sacred, so at least here the trees and plants were safe from the ravages of the poor who needed wood for their fires.

David stopped with a start at the sudden appearance of a suave *bonze* who had emerged from nowhere. The man invited them to join him in some tea and a pipe of opium. David was struck by the man's manners and politeness, but for once his courage failed and he stood his ground.

'Come on,' the lama insisted.

'No. I'm frightened of your large dogs,' replied David.

The lama frowned, perplexed. 'Dogs? Dogs?' he repeated. 'But we have no dogs.'

David smiled. 'No dogs! I have just heard the barking of a dog which made me tremble from head to foot. Listen!' All three listened. The bark boomed out again. 'There! I told you!' said David, vindicated.

'You heard a dog? But that is not a dog: it is a frog.'

'A frog!' retorted David in unbelief. 'A frog?'

'Yes,' the lama replied, 'the frog of the cascades. It is a large black frog which lives in the cascades of these mountains and it has a strong, deep voice. I suppose you could say its croak is like the bark of a dog.'

On the return journey to Nazareth David was surprised to find his strength had suddenly left him. He had not taken sufficient precaution against the sun and in his enthusiasm for new plants and animals he had overexerted himself; he was suffering from sunstroke. Every now and then he was forced to stop, unable to go on. During one of these enforced rests, Ouang, equally careless against the enervating sun, imprudently jumped into the cool waters of a nearby stream and even fell asleep there, as formerly he had on the back of a mule in Mongolia. It was David's watchful eye that prevented him losing his life.

The diary for the next day (17 July) records: 'The day is very hot again, and is spent preparing specimens. I feel very tired and sick from yesterday's sunstroke. Let us hope there will be no serious consequences.'

David was determined to find the 'barking' frog. After a few days' rest he set off for the pagoda at Ly Shan. The lamas were glad to let them have a room, and allowed them to cook the rice which formed their staple diet, along with rotted eggs, Chinese style, salted with garlic.

It was intriguing to find that the *bonzes* were not alone. They had several

The pagoda pointed dramatically into the sky
– a tribute to Chinese architectural skill.

young Chinese men staying with them. Evidently they were students who had come to enjoy the solitude of the lamas, away from the distractions and heat of the plains, to prepare for their examinations. The province of Kiangsi was known for the number of scholars and mandarins it provided for the Empire's civil service.

David was surprised to find that the students, who were from twenty to twenty-six years of age, studied by reading and chanting aloud, as if the noise would implant the facts on their memory better that way. David wondered, too, if this constant screaming from morning to night was not a contributory factor to the lung trouble so common among such students. That night he was violently ill. The pains in his stomach were unbearable and he was sick several times. What illness could this be? He could not think of anything untoward he had eaten or drunk.

On 15 August, the Feast of the Assumption, David and Thomè decided to go to Kiukiang for the festival. A torrential downpour overtook them, and they made for a nearby house. David remembered an earlier occasion in Mongolia when, drenched to the skin, he had begged shelter from the Chinese innkeeper but had received only the vilest abuse and was left to shiver in the cold. He knocked on the door; he was greeted courteously and invited in. The well-dressed and obviously well-educated Chinaman served them tea and offered the customary pipe. During a long conversation the women and young girls of the house found one pretext after another to enter the room to see what a *Siang-jen* (Westerner) looked like.

They were forced to remain in Kiukiang because of Ouang Thomè's illness: an intermittent fever, difficult to cure. It was probably due to the interminable vegetable diet of badly prepared gourds and cucumbers they had been living on. Or was it malaria? Ouang had no confidence in European medicine. He consistently refused the quinine David offered him, preferring to take crude Chinese medicines and, to David's dismay, drinking a great deal of native brandy.

During his stay at Nazareth David had added extensively to his collection. He had found nine or ten new species of mammals, thirty species of birds, sixty of fish, reptiles and batrachia; no less than 634 species of insects, and 194 species of plants. And, of course, *Rana latrans*. The barking of the frogs above the cacophony of the cicadas had divulged their hiding-places and David had been able to secure one of the species.

The 2 September was, indeed, a red-letter day. The steamer from Shanghai was arriving that day and as many missionaries as possible, including David, had found some excuse for being present at the bishop's residence on that day, when they hoped for letters and packets from relatives back home.

114

David was somewhat disappointed to have only one letter, but he was luckier than some, who would be returning empty-handed to their missions.

An official letter! What could this be? thought David as he opened the brown envelope. He looked at the bottom of the page: the letter was from Monseigneur Baldus, whom he had met so recently. He read from the top: the superior-general of the Vincentian Fathers was visiting the Chinese missions and wanted to meet David. Would David make every effort to return to Shanghai as soon as possible to meet Monseigneur Salvayre?

While David made his preparations to return to Shanghai he tried to figure out why he was being singled out for this appointment with the superior-general. Was he being recalled to Europe, to teach future young missionaries? No, not yet! That would break his heart; he had just started learning the flora and fauna of China. In view of the many missionaries murdered in recent months, had the superior-general decided to go back on his earlier decision giving David permission to make a second journey of scientific exploration?

Were his services more valuable, teaching at the College? Should he be spending more time on saving souls than on saving endangered species? He himself often had serious doubts as to whether scientific research was not taking up too much of his time. Often he would justify his choice to himself as when he wrote: 'My superiors found it right in view of the indirect value to religion for me to give my time for a while to work specially requested by the Government.'

A week later, leaving behind Ouang Thomè who was still very ill, David boarded the *Hirado* for the three-week trip back to Shanghai. During most of the journey David's mind was wracked with questions about the reason for his unexpected summons. Confined to the boat, with no exotic plants and animals to examine, the only explorations he could make were with his thoughts. Time and again he rehearsed the various possible scenarios that awaited him. His imagination went through the worst possible eventuality.

'There have been complaints,' the superior-general would begin.

'Complaints?' David would feign surprise.

'Yes. Complaints that you are spending too much time wandering around China, chasing butterflies and wild geese instead of saving souls.' How would he reply to that charge? 'I suggest you devote more time to your vocation and to evangelism.'

'But am I not doing just that? I live for – my whole life centres on – spreading the Gospel. That is why I came out here.'

David's mind went back to the Major Seminary in Bayonne where, as a young man of twenty, he had begun his studies for the priesthood. Two years

115

later, in 1848, he had entered the order of St Vincent de Paul. In 1850, then twenty-four years old, he had taken the three vows of poverty, chastity and obedience. He could still hear the voice of the archdeacon echoing down the cathedral, calling out his name: 'Armand David! Do you still wish to be ordained?'. His mother and father and brothers and sister were in the congregation. He remembered how he was so moved he could hardly blurt out the '*adsum*' in response to the archdeacon's call. He remembered lying prostrate before the high altar, so engrossed in his own prayers to be oblivious to the monotonous cadences of the bishop as he intoned the litany.

And then the bishop had laid his hands on his head. 'Let us beg of God, the Father Almighty, that He multiply heavenly gifts on this His servant, whom He has chosen for the office of Priesthood, and that what by His graciousness he undertakes, by His assistance he may attain.' Then he recalled being vested with the stole: 'Take thou the yoke of the Lord, for His yoke is sweet and His burden light.' He recalled holding out his hands while the bishop anointed his palms with the holy oils of catechumens in the form of a cross.

He thought affectionately of Sambdatchiemda, and of Ouang Thomè, of the many times when, in the most bleak and desolate of places, he had carried out the injunctions of the bishop: 'Receive the power to offer Sacrifice to God, and to celebrate Mass, both for the living and the dead.' He remembered all the emotions that gripped him as the bishop unfolded the chasuble, which until then had laid folded on his shoulder, with the words: 'May the Lord clothe thee with the robe of innocence.'

That letter he had written to Bishop Mouly in 1852, while he was teaching science at the College in Savona on the Italian Riviera – that would provide ammunition for his case:

> I am content here with my position and the occupations conform to my taste. I have nothing of which to complain, yet all the time I dream of Chinese missions. The more my natural tastes are satisfied the more I am strengthened in my first resolve. I fear I might lose the vocation for which I was confirmed and in which I was encouraged by my director, Fr Martin; indeed, for the past twelve years I am pursued with the thought of dying while working at the saving of unbelievers. It is this desire which caused me to become a priest and to come to the mission. I am getting on in years and am almost twenty-seven, and want to go to the Celestial Empire, Mongolia, and other similar places as soon as possible in order to learn

new languages, customs, and climates. Thank God my health is excellent and my always robust constitution will enable me to undergo the life, fatigue, and privations of a misssionary. However I cannot say the same of other qualities I wish I had. Alas! My desire to go to the missions is motivated in part by a desire to do penance, but also by the belief that since childhood God has called me to this.

And this was still his vocation: to share in the hard day-to-day work of the missionaries who for the past three centuries had tried to convert the vast population of the Far East to Christ.

'Then why don't you do that?'

Monseigneur Salvayre would reply. 'There are so few of us in the missions, and there is so much to do. The work of exploring any layman can do. Dispensing the Sacraments – is for priests.'

'But surely one can do both?' David would reply. 'Look at what Francis Xavier did. Look at what Matteo Ricci did. As long ago as 1598 the Jesuit astronomer and mathematician was preaching the faith at Emperor Wan-Li's court in Peking. Look at the great work Father Huc and Father Gabet did. Not only did they give us our first ideas of all those unexplored regions of Tartary and Tibet: they saved souls on the way as well. Yes, they saved my faithful guide Sambdatchiemda. They preached the words of Our Lord wherever they went – even in the Potala at Lhasa – at great danger to their lives.'

How David wished the venerable and saintly Monseigneur Mouly, with a flowing white beard which made him look more Chinese than the Chinese, would be there. He knew David well, and would speak for him. As soon as the Order had decided to agree to David's request to be sent to China, it was Bishop Mouly who had taken David to meet Mr Stanislas Juline, the great Chinese scholar and member of the Institute of France. Juline had been impressed by the knowledge and enthusiasm of the young man before him and, in turn, had introduced David to other members of the Academy of Sciences.

At that time very little was known about China, especially the more remote inland parts, and even less about its natural history. The members of the Academy had expressed the wish that maybe David could help fill that gap. It was with Bishop Mouly that he had first travelled out to China in 1864 on a five-month voyage, as the Suez Canal had not yet been opened.

David's heart sank as he heard the sad news, hardly before he had even disembarked at Shanghai. His saintly advocate was no more. There had never before been such huge crowds in Peking for the funeral of a foreigner: everyone loved the bishop.

It was with much misgiving that David met Monseigneur Salvayre, but all his pessimistic scenarios proved unwarranted. The superior-General had wanted David's views on establishing other colleges, specialising in science and mathematics, as did the College where David taught in Peking. Monseigneur Salvayre gave David full approval to continue his scientific work.

12

UP THE YANGTZE:
ORDEAL BY RAPID

David's explorations were held up by the unusually heavy rains that continued day after day, with consequent serious flooding. The Yangtze was too swollen to be navigable: it covered the northern plain of China as far as the eye could see. There were rumours that farther north the Hoang-Ho, the Yellow River, had overflowed and changed its bed over a considerable distance. It was thought that these overflow waters from the Hoang-Ho were now joining those of the Yangtze to form a vast inland sea. Scores of villages had been completely blotted out; thousands of peasants, unable to escape to high ground – which was very often non-existent – had drowned. The mission house at Kiukiang where David was staying was completely surrounded by the rising waters. Movement outside was possible only by boat. Finally, the waters even entered the house, bringing with them innumerable frogs, toads and fish. Even more to David's annoyance, the damp, humid conditions caused him to lose many specimens of plants and animals.

Every night carnival processions took place on the waters of the lake to appease the aquatic gods and pray for the floods to diminish. Paper lanterns of every size, shape and colour were placed on the waters to still the wrath of the gods. All this achieved was the spreading of the poisonous oil, *t'ung-yu*, derived from the nut of *Aleurites fordii* and used to light the lanterns, on the rising waters. The oil killed large numbers of fish, many of which were caught by the fishermen. This unusual circumstance enabled David to acquire specimens he would probably not have obtained otherwise.

Not until 13 October was David able to continue his journey up the Yangtze. He sailed on the *Hirado*, accompanied by four other missionaries who were returning to their mission stations in Szechwan and Yunnan provinces. The vast river was dotted with every type of craft – junks, sampans, rowing-boats, sailing-boats, and yet others being towed by ropes. Numerous rafts, laden with pine and spruce from the forests of Hunan and Szechwan, made their way down river to the sea. The next day the red sandstone and fine-grained granite buildings in the distance heralded the city of Hankow. The flooding of the Han River, swollen by the waters of the Yangtze, threatened to inundate the low-lying city.

David and the other missionaries could have made the trip to Chungking on one large boat. However, between Hankow and Shasi the Yangtze had so many turns and twists that the journey would have taken at least a fortnight, and they had already lost much time waiting for the floods to subside. They decided to travel by two smaller boats. Using the interconnecting lakes and canals they could reach Shasi, 175 miles (280 km) away, in eight days, although this would necessitate the disadvantage of having to change ship again at Shasi. Having reinforced their clothing by the purchase of padded vests for the coming cold, they set off in two boats for Shasi.

The boats were flat-bottomed, and caulked not with tar, but with the thick oil, *t'ung-yu*. They were decked over with boards held together with ropes instead of nails; the cabin was so small that one could not stand up straight. The boatmen slept under roofs of bamboo matting which they put up at night, either at the bow or stern of the boat. While two boatmen rowed, a third baled out the water which came in through the fissures in unnerving quantities. Soon they had left the wide river to enter a narrow canal leading to the lakes fed by the Han. Where the shores were distant the boatmen rowed, but where the canal was narrow they hauled the boat with ropes; sometimes the water was shallow enough for the boat to be punted along. There were few birds to be seen, but towards evening flights of wild ducks winged past.

That night David was violently ill with distressingly severe pains in his stomach. He took to his bunk, from which he had to rush at frequent intervals to vomit or evacuate his bowels. At one stage he passed out completely with the acute pain. He remembered the similar malady he had suffered around Kiukiang. He could not make out what it was. The thought of poison occurred to him. That was the usual way of doing away with people in China, and the people around him were hostile and suspicious. They believed him to be a western spy, travelling into the interior of the Empire to make maps or to prospect for precious metals. Several Fathers of his Order had been murdered by poisoning, indeed only recently Father Delamarre had been killed this way. He had been a remarkably excellent Chinese scholar, so much so that he had incurred the jealousy of certain mandarins, who bribed his servant to put poison in his tea. David spent a dreadful night, most of it in the toilet. However, the evacuations seemed to rid some of the poison from his system – if poison it was – and by the next day he did not feel as if he were about to die at any minute.

Occasionally the wind was strong enough for the boatmen to put up the sail, which gave them some respite from the hard labour of rowing. One day there was no wind at all: they rowed all day yet only covered 23 miles (37 km). All about them they could see the havoc wreaked by the floodwaters; in many places just the tops of houses, and occasionally just the top tier of a pagoda, were visible. Another day the wind was so strong it dashed the small flat boat against the opposite bank, almost overturning the little craft and spilling its precious cargo. This was on the ninth day of the ninth month in the Chinese calendar, and, as the local proverb prophesied, that was the day for storms and hurricanes, as was also the third day of the third month. They were glad to take shelter, pinned up against the inhospitable shore, their only companions a large dark-coloured heron and some blue magpies.

By evening the wind had subsided, and the local fishermen were venturing out in their low boats. David was surprised to see that these boats each held twenty to thirty cormorants. At a touch of his long pole the fisherman's cormorants would dive into the water and disappear completely, surfacing only either to breathe or to carry a fish between their beaks to their master. The birds had metallic rings round their necks which prevented the fish being swallowed. The fishermen would catch the cormorants by the neck, remove the fish from their beaks, then throw the birds back into the water. They obviously took great care of the birds. When they saw that their cormorants were tired they would put them back on their perches and leave them there for a long time to dry their plumage.

Next day David saw another form of fishing: a system of long bamboo poles raised and lowered immense square nets, in the centre of which were elongated ends shaped like reverse funnels or wicker fish baskets. Day and night an old man, woman or child sat in a cabin alongside the nets, raising and lowering them periodically.

One day towards the end of October the interminable interconnecting lakes and canals finally came to an end and they were back on the Yangtze: they had reached Shasi. Now came the onerous task of shipping their baggage on to a bigger boat. But, as David had long since found out, nothing happens quickly in China. The *Shan-liang*, the unavoidable intermediaries who hired boats, said it would be several days before a boat could be arranged. Smiling, the chief *Shan-liang* added that, of course, for certain considerations things could be speeded up. He was obviously a very successful businessman: his open mouth displayed a fortune in gold teeth.

David and his colleagues decided to spend the intervening time at a mission in the old walled city of Kingchow (now Kiangling). They finally reached the mission house and chapel, the Kung-kuan, only to find that Father

Fishing with cormorants. The birds had
metallic rings around their necks to prevent
the fish from being swallowed.

Lo, the Chinese priest, possibly overawed at the prospect of meeting strange
Western priests, had gone off into the wilds in search of conversions. There
was little chance of success, since the population was very hostile to foreigners
and even more so to Christians. There was a small Christian community living
near the mission house who were all very poor, making their living through
the manufacture of oiled paper umbrellas. David moved into the empty

mission house. One of the Christians volunteered his services to cook for David; he was a good cook, and even more adroit at swindling the good priests on the price and quality of the provisions he was buying.

The city of Kingchow was surrounded by canals, most of which were almost overflowing their banks. It was a very ancient city, several thousand years old, since Confucius spoke of it as already old in his day. Among the population were some Tartar-Manchus, living in a separate quarter of the city, who were employed by the government as mercenaries. For their services the government provided them with pay and rice and good land, for the upkeep of themselves and their horses. They had intermarried with the local Chinese and one could not now tell the difference between them and the native Chinese, except that the women let their feet grow to a natural size.

The whole countryside round Kingchow was obviously very fertile. There were rich fields of *pai-ts'ai* (radishes), carrots and sugar-cane, interspersed here and there by burial mounds and tombs. That year the rice harvest had been particularly good and David would often see processions of grateful people on their way to the pagoda, or *miao*, to render their thanks.

At long last final travel arrangements were completed, and David and his companions set off for the rendezvous with the boat. As part of the contract David was obliged to carry cases of tools and arms to a European armourer in the services of the Great Mandarin of Kweichow. Stumbling over obstacles in the dark, with the porters staggering under their loads, they eventually made out the outlines of the boat. On board, the missionaries found that several of their belongings had 'disappeared' en route. Knowing the Chinese, David was quite convinced the whole situation had been prearranged with the collusion of the *Shan-liang* and possibly of the ship's captain as well.

The boat that was to take them farther up the Yangtze was a fairly large craft. The unusually high prow in the front of the boat was for protection against the jagged rocks when they came into the swirling, bubbling waters of the rapids. The captain was a young man; it was his mother who seemed to be the boss. In between puffs on her opium pipe, the cadaverous-looking woman, her health – and her purse – ruined by the drug, would shout obscene orders to the crew. The crew consisted of about twenty members, who would travel as far as Ichang, where other boatmen, more experienced with the vagaries of the river, would take the boat as far as Chungking.

The song of the boatmen as they rowed in unison was something to be heard: first one of the men would sing out, at as high a pitch as he could manage, a few long tremulous notes, like the Irrintzina of the Basque smugglers, then the crew would answer with a formidable *heou*, ascending or descending chromatically according to circumstances. If the boat was under

A boat for shooting the many dangerous
rapids on the Yangtze River. The high prow in
front was for protection against jagged rocks.

sail, and the wind threatened to die down, the boatmen would whistle in
unison to invoke the god of winds.

Whenever the strong current, or *changpo*, as the boatmen called it,
slowed the boat down to less than walking speed, the passengers would get out,
not only to lessen the weight in the boat, but also to stretch their limbs after
sitting cross-legged, Buddha-like, for hour after hour. On one such occasion
they left the path that followed the river and turned inland so as to avoid the
town of Chiang-k'ou, where their presence would only excite the hostile
population, aiming to catch up with the boat later. This pleased David as it
would give him an opportunity to study the plants and animals of the
countryside. They intended to skirt the lake ahead of them and reach the river

higher up. But as they walked their pace got slower as they became more and more enmeshed in an inextricable maze of swamp. They slithered to their knees in the black mud. It would soon be dusk. David enquired about the route: it would take at least twenty-four hours to make the circuit. He advised retracing their steps, but the other missionaries were loath to do so and decided to accomplish the impossible through energy and agility.

As night approached the lake appeared even longer as they tried to pick out the end of it. Then the rain came down and it became impossible to continue in the quagmire. They decided to retreat, tired and extremely hungry. Guided by the directions of a good peasant they finally found themselves in the town of Chiang-k'ou, the very place they had hoped to avoid. They crossed the streets as quickly as possible. Fortunately, the heavy rain had driven the people off the streets and kept them in the dens with their drink and opium. They reached the road where they had left the boat that morning and hurried on. Then, catastrophe! A wide canal, through which the lake emptied into the Yangtze, blocked their way. Some frantic shouting brought out a boatman. He was reluctant to cross the canal at night but the promise of a worthwhile reward tempted him.

They settled into the boat. While the boatman heaved on the oars, the now very concerned missionaries considered their plight: they had no money, and their valuables were on the large boat in the care of Father Turgis. Surreptitiously they searched their pockets in the hope of finding something. Father Provôt whispered that he had found some cash, but not amounting to a tip even, let alone the fares. The boat struck the far shore. While Father Provôt searched majestically in his pockets for the equivalent of a few centimes in cash, the others, including David, beat a hasty retreat into the enveloping shadows. Father Provôt scampered up to join them just as the poor boatman realised what had happened. They hurried along, the foulest of obscene language shattering the peace of the still night behind them.

They pressed on but there was no sign of their boat. Surely the boatmen would have waited when they didn't return earlier? But they remembered they were in China. They quickened their pace, but there was no boat. Father Provôt, who spoke the best Chinese of the group, asked for news of the boat. Those who had seen it said it had gone much farther up. He implored them to guide them or at least lend them a proper lantern. '*Lao-pan*,' Father Provôt called out as they passed any houses where a light still burned. '*Lao-pan*,' the loud stentorian voice rang out. 'Have pity on poor lost travellers. Come and guide us to a mandarin boat. We shall pay you well.' Although he used the title *Lao-pan*, which is only accorded to people of some importance, he received neither lantern nor guide.

125

They hurried on, often stumbling and falling over each other. Father Bompas, who had been strolling along a high path ruminating philosophically, suddenly disappeared from sight. A loud cry came up from the field about 12 feet (3·5 m) below. It took them some time to extricate the now not-so-philosophical Father from the soft mud of the paddy-field. He was considerably shaken, but apart from a few bruises and cuts was able to carry on, this time his mind more on where he was placing his feet. The situation was becoming desperate. The unnerving thought crossed David's mind that the boat, with all their valuables aboard, might just carry on, leaving them utterly stranded in anything but hospitable country; it would only take a few seconds for the crew to shove young Father Turgis overboard. Eventually they reached an abandoned house which blocked the way. To the left the river sped by and to the right was a marsh; there was nothing to do but stop. The house had a roof which projected about two feet, under which lay a few bundles of sorghum. Very hungry and very fatigued, sweating and soaking wet, they huddled against each other and tried to sleep. But the cold biting wind ensured that there was no rest.

About two hours later their prayers were answered. Two flickering lights came nearer and nearer. It was two Chinese, who had decided to take up the offer of a cash reward. David was mightily relieved and took back the epithets he had hurled at the hard-hearted Chinese who had earlier scorned their pleas for help. The party struggled on for another three hours, stumbling and swearing as they went, and as the first light of day was breaking over the hills they reached a tea-garden. The two guides prevailed on the owner to open up, tea was heated and *chao-chiu* (sorghum brandy) was served. The guides preferred the latter, one of them so much so that he was soon drunk, evidently not for the first time, but despite many falls he and his colleague led them eventually to the boat. The missionaries were glad to see the frightened Father Turgis alive and well, and their valuables were safe. After a good meal, and more *chao-chiu*, the two guides got their *tiao* (long strings of cash) and left. Before leaving they each managed to pilfer two additional strings of *tiao*.

As the boat glided along the river, they caught sight of the high mountains rising behind Chih-chiang. Tallow trees grew in abundance. Father Provôt pointed out the wax trees, now leafless; little insects raised on this plant produced the fine transparent wax so highly regarded in China. The hills gradually became more thickly wooded, the whitewashed houses standing out attractively against the green vegetation, and surrounded by orange trees and hemp palms, as well as large banana trees, the first David had seen.

The rain persisted most days and nights. Unlike their countrymen from the north who stopped travelling or doing any outside work while it rained, the boatmen here seemed not to mind the rain, continuing to row or haul the boat.

On November 11th they shot their first rapid: they were approaching Ichang, notorious for its dangerous waters. As the boat shot over the rapid they were spun around dizzily but the crewmen, using their long oars to stave the boat off the jagged rocks, soon had the boat under control. It was a foretaste of things to come. They watched with admiration as a 'boat' of inflated ox-hides, carrying wool and hides on the tremendous journey from the pastures of Lake Koko Nor to the sea, was poled skilfully through the rapids. In the distance they could see the high tower announcing the city of Ichang. As they neared the Ichang gorge the tall precipitous mountains came down to a pointed 'V' through which they passed with great care. At midday they passed a pagoda like an eagle's nest perched overlooking the river on the pointed top of a mountain, which had been worn to a peak by the abrasive action of the water over aeons of years.

The boat stopped at Ichang. According to the agreement the captain had the right to stop there for two days to add to his crew. Many more men would be required to haul the boat through the larger rapids farther up river. While these tiresome but necessary arrangements were being made David climbed one of the mountains, 1,600 feet (490 m) above the Blue River. Below him lay

As the boat shot over the rapid it was spun around dizzily, but the crewmen used their long oars to avoid the jagged rocks.

At the entrance to the Ichang gorge, notorious for its dangerous rapids, the mountains came down to a pointed 'V'.

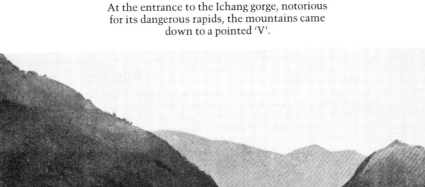

the partly walled city, separated into two parts by an arm of the Yangtze. Here were bamboos and shaddock with huge acid fruits, giving the landscape a semitropical appearance. Pyrethrums, violets, clematis, abelia, asters, white chrysanthemums and curious gentians David had not seen before abounded everywhere. He saw several ferns that were new to him. Close to the houses were large willows and a kind of laurel with white bark and black fruits.

While looking for insects under some stones he found two tiny adult frogs he had never seen before. They were grey-red in colour, their backs marked with brown, angular lines, symmetrical on both sides. David named this tailless pygmy batrachian of China *Ranina symetrica*. It was considerably smaller than the *Rana latrans* of the Kiangsi cascades and the big frog of the rice-fields, the *Rana tigrina*.

Birds were conspicuous by their absence. Only the kite made its appearance, gliding lazily over the city and the boats, sometimes coming to rest on the masts.

David was glad to reach the boat and rest his weary legs. The sun set under a beautiful, clear sky, which was emblazoned every now and then by spectacular falling stars. Everyone laughed as Father Bompas carefully lifted up his bedcover before turning in for the night. It was not unknown to find a coffin complete with contents under one's bunk.

Many new boatmen joined the boat the next morning, each carrying his makeshift bed and a tiny bundle.

The peace of the day was spoilt by long and sometimes acrimonious haggling between Father Gennevoise, who was acting as *tang-chia*, or treasurer, for the group of missionaries, and the young captain, who was demanding more cash for the trip, although he had already been more than generously recompensed. He asked for a new contract, and lamented and wept in concert with his mother. But the good treasurer was not fooled by these carryings-on.

As they made their way to the Ichang gorge, the road or towpath became increasingly difficult for the men hauling the boat. Three or four men, leaning forward shoulder to shoulder, with wooden frames across their chests to which were attached long ropes connected to the mast, hauled the heavy load. They climbed and jumped like monkeys to surmount the tricky parts.

David sat bolt upright from reading his Breviary. The crack was like a rifle-shot. At the bow of the boat stood two *chiourme*, each holding a huge whip in his hand. David could not believe his eyes as he saw the two raise their right arms and then bring the whips cracking across the backs of the hauliers, dripping with rain and sweat and now blood.

'Hey,' shouted David, as he stood up in anger. 'You can't do things like that. Stop it.' The *chiourme* glared down at David and showed their disap-

Three men, leaning forward shoulder to
shoulder, hauled the heavy boat.

proval by lashing the hauliers again, and then again for good measure. The
Chinese could often be cruel and heartless.

Father Provôt pulled David back to his seat. He explained that this was
the custom of the country, justified by the exceptional difficulties caused by
the ravines and gorges. The hauliers did not complain.

The atmosphere became dark and foreboding as the high, overhanging
mountains constricted the mighty river from a width of several miles in places
to a mere 200 yards (185 m) at the entrance to the gorges. Hauling was no
longer possible and the men clambered aboard. The wind caught the newly
erected sails and they glided slowly and with difficulty between the rock faces.
To David's surprise the river flowed slowly: hemming in so huge a volume of
water into such a narrow constriction would normally have catapulted the
waters through the narrow opening at a great speed. The only explanation
seemed to be that the river was very, very deep there.

David was struck by the fact that quite different species of plants grew on
the two banks, separated as they were by the deep river. His mind recalled the
instances Darwin had mentioned in his *Origin of Species* – as, for example, in

the Galapagos islands – where species had evolved differently because of differing environmental conditions. He was now observing differently evolved varieties of once-identical species resulting from the different conditions on the separated banks.

Passing through the gorge was an experience: the scenery was of surpassing beauty. From the banks of the river, peaks rose several hundred feet sheer out of the water, cascades falling down their faces in mists, etching grottoes in the vertical walls.

The wind presently fell and the boat was rowed on silent waters, resembling a subterranean river. In the afternoon they passed the customs post without too much aggravation, a few gifts handed here and there speeding up the formalities. The customs officers warned that only a fortnight ago no less than twenty-three boats had been destroyed within the space of ten days by a single rock hidden by the water just beyond the customs post.

The sheer rock faces resounded to the incessant singing of the rowers. Although the banks of the gorges were very steep, they were cultivated by the Chinese wherever a field could be made. Little terraces were held up by walls, similar to the amphitheatre-like steps of Liguria in Italy, where olive trees are grown. Orange trees, shaddock and hemp palms were common here. The branches of bamboo, with their bright green, elegant foliage, curved downward like some of the firs, and the common pine crowned all the heights. Even in places which

The Lukan gorge. The atmosphere became dark and foreboding as high overhanging mountains constricted the mighty river to a width of a mere 200 yards (185 m).

seemed quite inaccessible the trees had had their lower branches stripped off for firewood.

Before reaching the several rapids marked by the Huang-ling-miao pagoda, the voyagers all disembarked to lighten the boat. The rapids ran between massive granite blocks which obstructed the river in several places.

Entrance to the Hsin-t'an rapids, the most dangerous
rapids of all. It was here that eleven of David's colleagues
had been wrecked three years before.

The next day the clouds hung heavy on the mountains. They set off early so as not to be delayed by other boats, which were hauled one by one and at long intervals so as to prevent any mishaps to other boats should the ropes break, as they were frequently wont to do. The tow-ropes were about 600 feet (185 m) long and yet only the width of two fingers, yet they had to be exceptionally strong, strong enough to take the strain of sometimes as many as eighty hauliers pulling the boat through the more turbulent rapids. The ropes were made from bamboo braided and twisted together, and unfortunately they got frayed easily from rubbing against the rocks. At one bend in the river the party came upon a massive rapid formed by heaps of granite rocks. Clinging on to the sharp and slippery rocks were the unfortunate victims of the most recent shipwreck. It was pitiful to hear their cries for help, but the raging waters and the jagged lumps of granite made it impossible for any help to get near them.

Soon they passed the fine pagoda of San-tou-p'ing, and were glad to see the high, black mountains of Wushan ahead of them. But there were more rapids yet to traverse. The three Hsin-t'an rapids were considered by Chinese navigators to be the most dangerous of all. It was here that eleven missionaries of the foreign mission had been wrecked three years ago: that day they covered only a third of a mile (0·5 km). The delay was due not only to the rapids – the captain took on board any merchandise he could salvage from the wrecks that were littered round the granite rocks.

By nightfall they had reached the Hsin-t'an rapids. A long village stretched out on the right bank; another long village stretched out on the left bank. They could see cotton and other debris scattered on the beach from recent shipwrecks. The houses of two large towns clinging to the mountain-sides were supported by means of numerous wooden columns. These towns had come into being not only because of the frequent shipwrecks that occurred there, but also because of the necessity of maintaining extra hauliers to traverse the rapids. Again, the land was cultivated to the very tops of the mountains.

They experienced several frightening moments as their boat was spun around and around like a tiny matchbox in a massive whirlpool between two huge, menacing rocks. The boatmen struggled against the furious current, hauling on two ropes with all their strength before they finally succeeded in pulling the boat out of the maelstrom. How had they missed the rocks and the wreckage of other boats? David had been sure his last moments had come. When they finally reached calmer waters the boatmen swore that devils had agitated and disturbed the waters.

Approaching Kong-tcheou the shores of the Yangtze drew closer to each other like menacing walls, the bottoms more worn away than the tops, looking as if they would tumble into the river at any moment. The boat tied up for the night at Patung (the eight caverns), whose houses, raised on colonnades of poles and trees, resembled those in the high valleys of the Alps.

The weather was growing noticeably colder. It was now the third week of November – winter. The mountains at the entrance to the Wushan gorge were covered with snow. In addition to the many perils of a journey into the interior of China there were the extremes of climate to contend with. In summer in Peking, at 40° latitude, the heat equalled that of Cairo, at 30° latitude; in winter it was as cold as Uppsala in Sweden, at 60° latitude. Finally they reached Wushan. The mountains bordering and confining the river rose perpendicularly out of the water to a height of 2,000 – 3,000 feet (610 – 920 m). Stunted bushes and trees grew on the immense walls, safe from any woodcutter's axe.

Beyond Wushan they had to stop again, to await their turn to be hauled up the short but very steep Hsia-ma-t'an rapids. When their turn came it took more than eighty men more than half an hour to move the boat just 15 feet (4·5 m). Just then loud shouts and indescribable confusion erupted, everyone held on to anything at hand as a large boat, propelled by the whirlpool, came hurtling towards them, completely out of control. Some of the crewmen

A magnificently built pagoda, admirable in its ornate architecture and design.

saw the danger and acted just in time to stave off a disastrous collision, parrying the onrushing boat sufficiently to lessen the full force of impact.

They were some 20 miles (32 km) from the city of Kweichow (now Fengkieh). A massive rock, notorious for the many shipwrecks it had caused, jutted at least 15 feet (4·5 m) out of the water. In olden times the emperor had given orders for all such rocks that obstructed navigation to be blown up. However the locals prevented any blasting by gunpowder because they superstitiously believed that that would cause the whole city of Kweichow to be destroyed by fire.

At Kweichow David and a few of the other missionaries left the boat and went overland to visit Father Vincot, who had lived in China for twenty years.

There was little he did not know about the language and customs of the people. Kweichow was evidently a prosperous city: it was surrounded by fine walls; the roads were handsomely paved; the population was extensive and most were well-off. David and his companions were all delighted to meet another European, surrounded as they were by people unsympathetic, even hostile, to them.

The seemingly new building in which Father Vincot lived had had all its woodwork devoured by termites or white ants; nevertheless, they were all glad to sleep in a building after so many nights spent on the boat. Even though the many boatmen slept in a small boat that was towed behind the large one, one could not help smelling the opium they smoked, seemingly all through the night. Father Vincot was a mine of information. He told them that the rebellion in the province had begun because the government had insisted on payment of exploitation rights long after the once-rich mines had been exhausted, on the grounds that in accordance with Chinese laws these rights were granted in aeternum! Rather than open new mines that might soon become exhausted, the local people left them untouched, thus depriving everybody of much valuable revenue. David was also interested to learn about the fossils the venerable old priest had collected. The Chinese pulverised fossil bones for their native *materia medica*. He discovered that some few days' journey north of Kweichow the pine forests hid many rare and exotic birds and animals, including a type of green monkey, the tragopan, and several kinds of pheasant.

The following morning David was pleased to find some large, handsome pistachio trees in the mission garden. He collected some of the ripe seeds to send to the Botanical Museum in Paris. In the afternoon they returned to the boat, but it was no longer there. It had moored further up the river after passing the customs formalities. To reach it they had to pass extensive markets which had been established temporarily on the beach, in order to be near the numerous travellers. Before reaching the boat they had to run the usual gauntlet of obscene abuse and vile epithets from the hostile onlookers.

That evening David was intrigued by some fine music near the boat. It was a visitation by the *hoa-niang*, the river prostitutes, who plied their trade by going from one boat to another, travelling in small covered skiffs decorated with coloured lanterns. The ladies were all painted and decked out in their finery, singing and playing the guitar to their pimps' accompaniment on the violin. When the captain informed the ladies of fortune who his passengers were, however, the music stopped as they made off for other more likely customers. In his diary David wrote:

During the more than six years that I have lived in China, I must say, in praise of this Empire, that I have never before run across these unfortunate temptresses. But there are certain cities where bad morals and traditions are hereditary, and the rich city of Kweichow, where many employees of the imperial customs and numerous boatmen and travellers pass continually, has a sad reputation in this respect. The same is said of Canton and other ports. Man is more or less corrupt everywhere, but even in the heart of paganism there is a great difference between the different countries. In China, as a rule, the boldness and ostentation of vice are fortunately much more infrequent than might be expected. Modesty and decency are respected, at least outdoors. Moreover, almost everyone marries young and has a high regard for the honour of the family, so there are few people to indulge in dissipation; and (need it be said?) certain deviations are much rarer here than in unchristian Europe!

The next day their boat followed behind thirteen boats transporting an important mandarin and his suite from Peking to Szechwan to preside at the baccalaureate examinations. The horses that David could see walking in single file beside the river obviously belonged to the scholarly magistrate. The party was informed that higher up the river a large boat had been shipwrecked that very morning with the loss of many lives; not very cheering news. The mandarin boats were seldom involved in such accidents: they were better provided with men and equipment and they were always less heavily laden. Some of the boats David had seen were so weighted down the water was almost coming into them. It did not take much to cause them to capsize and sink.

On the first day of December they reached Yun-yang, where they stopped. David took the opportunity to visit the mission. Yun-yang was a fairly large city but without walls, built in the form of an amphitheatre; he was surprised to find such fine paved streets. Father Lo, the local Chinese priest, who had studied at the seminary at Muping, was able to tell him a lot about the flora and fauna of that unexplored region where David was heading. That evening the missionaries were greeted by the local Christians who had come to visit the *Shen-fu* (spiritual fathers). From their bundles they pulled out oranges, mandarins, enormous lemons and shaddocks, which they dared not be seen giving in daytime: the local populace was very hostile to Christianity.

The city of Wanhsien, where they later stopped, was one of the prettiest places David had ever set eyes on. Staircases, bridges, tombs, were all made of the most beautiful cut stones; even the roads were paved with them. The city was as prosperous as its morals were poor.

While returning to the boat David and his colleagues were spotted by some local people. They were soon surrounded by an angry, ill-intentioned crowd, who began hurling vile insults at them: 'kill the dogs'. To call anyone a dog, rabbit or tortoise, all symbols of impurity, was the most serious insult one could inflict. David explained their purpose was peaceful, only to further enrage the mob, who then began stoning the missionaries. They had little option but to beat a fast retreat to the boat.

As they continued their journey up the Yangtze, the country became greener and prettier all the time. The houses were for the most part hidden under thick foliage of bamboo, oranges, thuya and sacred fig trees. Sugar-cane fields appeared here and there on the hills. David would often see men carrying baskets filled with the gold-bearing sand collected along the banks; others would be busy washing the sand.

One evening, hardly had David begun to sleep on the large boat, while the rowers slept or smoked opium on their smaller one behind, when he was woken by the strange groans of one of the boatmen, whose cries resembled those of a dog on a leash. The other boatmen maintained he had hydrophobia; that he was mad. David gave him some medicine which seemed to soothe him. But next morning the supposedly mad man was in a pitiful state. He complained that his stepfather, who was the master helmsman, owed him money which he refused to return. For his part, the stepfather beat him with the utmost harshness at every possible opportunity. The young man had thrown himself into the river on more than one occasion to drown himself or to quench the *ch'i*, or fire, that burned within him. To the Chinese *ch'i* meant a kind of sudden spleen which seized them when they repressed themselves after having been insulted or deeply wronged. David had seen people die of it within twenty-four hours.

The next evening, while the boat was moored along the bank and the boatmen were finishing their rice, and David was finishing his prayers, the sick man, who had had his hands tied to his feet to prevent him throwing himself into the water and who had been left naked and shivering at the end of the boat, managed to heave himself to the edge of the boat and overboard into the raging water, where he was carried away by the current. Neither his stepfather nor any of his comrades made any attempt to rescue him. David caught sight of the poor man only when he was far away. This was too much for him; he angrily admonished them for their callousness, and was told in reply that they would burn fireworks in the dead man's honour.

A white tower built on a high hill to the left announced the approach to Fengtu. On the bank opposite the tower was a large beach of rocks and pebbles, where there had formerly been a small town. However, the town had been abandoned because devils in human form were said to haunt the place. A magnificently built pagoda adorned the summit of a pretty conical hill over-looking Fengtu, the ornate architecture and design of which was admirable even from a distance. The body of a deified saint with a gilded face was preserved in this sanctuary. The Chinese boatmen believed that no boat could navigate the rapids here without the saint's blessing, and, accordingly, burnt many fireworks in honour of the saint.

They passed the village of Li-shih-chen where the houses were remark-able not only for their whiteness but because they had beams and small joists crossed and inserted into the walls as in David's own Basque country. But David's thoughts of home were soon rudely interrupted by shouts and general pandemonium: the hawser had broken and the boat was drifting towards the ubiquitous granite rocks. However, with the assistance of two other boats the situation was saved.

Here the river curved into a large arc. David took the opportunity of travelling overland to Fowling, where the foreign missions had a station. Fowling was situated on the side of a mountain that sloped down to where the Yangtze joined the Pengshui (now Ch'ien Chiang) River, which was large and navigable, though very treacherous, its rapids and whirlpools showing little mercy to boats. The boats here had a special shape, pointed and raised at the two ends, and provided with a double rudder in the form of an enormous oar at each end. In some of the rapids the whirlpools were so violent that boats simply disappeared completely.

As he journeyed, David was pleased to see that the trees – thuya, oak and ash – were allowed to grow to a reasonable height before being chopped down: this was to provide the long timbers needed for building the sloops. Flocks of white herons abounded on the river. At Fowling David was told of the black monkey of Kweichow, which is very large, with a long tail, and extremely difficult to catch.

Next day they had an exciting drama. The slender rope hauling the boat had caught against some jagged rocks under the water and had been cut. The current shot the boat out into the river. They were fortunate to meet a boat passing in the opposite direction which was able to catch the runaway boat. So many rocks, so many wrecks! David wondered if he would ever reach Chung-king; there were still many rapids to negotiate.

It was now mid-December, and very cold, but that day they made much

A boat in a rapid, with bow sweep ready for use.

faster progress. The boat was now much lighter since 30 – 40 hundredweight (1·5 – 2 tonnes) of merchandise had been unloaded during the night, and each day hauliers would leave the boat as they reached their homes.

They passed the market town of San-pei-t'o, with its houses built like hen-houses perched on long poles, where the fishermen were bartering russet eels with narrow tails. Fortifications looked down from the tops of flat summits: refuges in times of trouble, where the local people would go with their possessions to be safe from the harassment of the many bandits, brigands and rebels that roamed the hills.

The river was now so wide and shallow the boat was hauled by a rope over 1,500 feet (450 m) long. They passed a boat like their own which had just been wrecked, having been hit and holed by a smaller boat out of control. That evening their boat waited to be joined by others. It was a point in the river where it was easy for the freshwater pirates to plunder any boats travelling singly.

David began to feel ill. The diary for 16 December records: 'I begin to feel very tired, morally and physically, and it seems as if this tyrannical navigation will never end.' He had barely fallen asleep when he was rudely aroused by loud shouting and screaming. It was the freshwater pirates robbing the boats around them.

Early next morning they reached the very large rapid Y-lo-dre, full of violent whirlpools. Again they were spun around several times as the boatmen struggled against the maelstrom and the protruding rocks that added considerably to the hazards. No sooner had they reached the comparative safety of calmer water than another boat which had broken loose from its hauliers bore down on them, carried on the strong current. A collision would mean certain death for everyone; no one could swim against that strong undertow and avoid being swallowed up in the eye of the whirlpool. Miraculously the two boats only grazed each other, all the petrified passengers holding on for grim life.

Freshwater pirates plundering whatever could be found.

139

Accused before a magistrate. For Chinese
converts to Christianity, life was very hard.

That same afternoon they saw the two cities of Kiangpeh and Chungking,
separated by a big river flowing from the north. Junks and boats of every
description were tied up along the shore. Against the dark green of orange trees
and other evergreens the whitewashed houses stood out attractively, if they
were not entirely hidden by clumps of bamboo. The two wealthy cities were
the centres of a considerable population amounting to half a million.

David disembarked at Chungking. Here, too, as in almost all China, the
people were hostile to foreigners and particularly to Christians. In Chungking,
as soon as a man adopted Christianity, like the lepers of biblical times, he was
completely ostracised, forbidden entry to all houses, deprived of all employ-
ment and of every means of livelihood. Christians were persecuted, attacked
and even murdered and burnt to such an extent that the good Fathers had been
constrained to restrict their work of evangelisation. Monseigneur Desflèches,

the apostolic vicar of eastern Szechwan, had sent instructions that the priests were to be as unobtrusive as possible and if they did travel in the city they should only do so in covered chairs so as not to excite the malevolent curiosity of the Chinese. Slowly and patiently, the porters bore David up the very steep stone spiral steps, like Jacob's ladder, that led to Monseigneur Desflèches's residence. At the top of the steps David's barometer recorded a height of 891 feet (271·5 m).

The Monseigneur's residence was a large Chinese house constructed of wood, with all the rooms on one floor. During a riot some six years earlier the pagans had razed the former episcopal residence to the ground.

Before long David was suffering from the notoriously humid climate, which provided rain more than half the days in the year. The sky was usually cloudy or foggy even without the thick pall of smoke that covered the city

The great wall of Chungking with the gate
towers. David was carried by porters up the
very steep stone spiral steps to Monseigneur
Desflèches's residence.

141

from the coal burnt there. It was said that most of the time half the inhabitants of Chungking were ill.

From Monseigneur Desflèches and Father Favan, who had lived in the province for more than thirty years, David obtained valuable information about the region to which he was going. Father Favan told David that as a result of keeping to the local custom of drinking tea without sugar he had suffered such insomnia that for a period of twelve years he had not been able to sleep and had almost gone out of his mind. It was only by using opium and abstaining scrupulously from tea that he had been able to sleep again and recover his health. They advised David that if it was rare plants and animals that he was after he should head for the independent principality of Muping. To get there he must first travel to Chengtu, the capital of Szechwan. He could get to Chengtu either by river or overland; by river the trip would take thirty days; by land only ten. David decided to go by land, sending his heavier baggage on by boat, in the care of the young missionaries he had been travelling with.

13

CHENGTU AND SURROUNDS

David made arrangements for the trip to the ancient walled city of Chengtu, the capital of Szechwan province, which for years had been an outpost of the caravan trade. There were no proper roads, and hence no carriages or wagons; no mules, donkeys or horses were used for transport. Everything was carried on men's backs. In accordance with his bishop's injunction he would travel in a covered chair so as not to arouse any hostile curiosity. David bought himself a chair and hired three men for carrying it and three others for his baggage and bedding and that of his faithful Ouang Thomè. The porters were all strapping men, who would travel a minimum of 10 miles (16 km) a day. By custom he would give the chair to the porters on arrival at Chengtu. In addition every two days he would give each porter a present and a tip and at the end of the trip each would receive 900 cash (about 1 ounce – 28 g – of silver) as a present and 3,600 cash (about three ounces – 85 g – of silver) as wages. David arranged to draw the cash at Chengtu. Carrying it with him was a sure way of never reaching Chengtu alive, especially as it was now nearing the end of the Chinese year, a time of great and often riotous festivities.

At the end of December David and his party set off, hoping to reach Chengtu in ten or twelve days. The road leading out of Chungking was at first paved and about 4 feet (1·2 m) wide but as they climbed up the mountains the road got narrower and narrower. It became more a series of steps cut into the mud, which was a quagmire because of the heavy rain. David often descended from the chair to lessen the burden of his porters, but they seemed to resent that, evidently not used to any such gestures of kindness from their usual Chinese customers. In this mandarin-trodden country the people were used to harsh treatment from the mandarins and looked on leniency as a sign of weakness.

At intervals they would pass men carrying coal on their backs. David was intrigued to see the bamboo plants ready to flower having never seen this before. Chinese bamboos only flower once and then the whole grove, being of the same age, dies. The porters told him that the white bears, the legendary *pei-hsuing* he had heard of, fed on this bamboo. A large buzzard with a white rump joined them on their trek. Finches and wagtails winged their way past. David recognised the whistle of the mandarin blackbird that he had first seen in Hankow.

Travel by sedan chair.

They passed a porcelain factory where water-power was used to drive machinery for breaking up the white sandstone which abounded everywhere. They also passed many people whose skins were as white as that of a foreigner. So perhaps David could pass himself off as one of the local inhabitants. They were glad, especially the porters, to reach the town of Lai-feng-i, where they stopped for the night.

Along the route stood several very handsome triumphal arches, constructed from enormous blocks of the white sandstone, worked with great artistry and delicacy. The fine carvings on the arches, which rose to 30 feet (9 m) or more, bore comparison with anything the great European sculptors had produced, whether Greek or Italian. These arches, or *p'ai-lou*, were erected by rich families either to perpetuate the memory of an act of charity, or more often to praise the virtue and abnegation of a young girl or widow who refused to marry in order to devote herself wholly to her old parents or orphaned relatives. Among the paving stones underneath the arches he often saw fossil shells, remnants of very ancient marine life.

Torrential rain forced them to an early halt. That night it snowed heavily, but next day was fine and they were able to continue, passing through low, cultivated hills. David observed an unknown bird, not reported before by any naturalist. It resembled a small version of the European blackbird, but was white at the base and sides. He named the new species *Dromolea imprevisa*.

David ate with the porters, but only pure rice: he could not stomach the salted and peppered pieces of carrot and turnip they used for seasoning. That evening he allowed himself the luxury of an egg and some pork, the only meat obtainable.

A fine stone bridge, with a plank floor and a roof, enabled them

Triumphal arches, or *p'ai-lo*, worked with great artistry from enormous blocks of white sandstone rising to 30 feet (9 m) or more, erected in memory of self-denying young women and widows.

to traverse a wildly raging river that led to the village of Huang-kuo-shu ('tree with yellow fruit'). Snow covered the thatched roofs; the tops of the mountains, too, were all white. They passed more triumphal arches, made of red and white sandstone, as well as huge plaques bearing the names of all the generous people who had contributed to the construction of the road, which was completely paved with huge slabs of sandstone.

The streams in the valleys were used for turning mills that made paper

A water mill on the Chengtu Plain, where
paper or cord were made from crushed
bamboo. Bamboo and wood houses, with
walls and roof made of thatch, were built
above the horizontal wheels.

from bamboo. The year-old shoots of bamboo were first cut and then macer-
ated in warm water by water-driven hammers and reduced to a fibre or a pulp,
depending on whether cord or paper was to be made. David was intrigued at
seeing yet another form of fishing – by otter. The ingenious Chinese had
trained otters to catch fish from the waters of the deeper rivers.

The few shops they encountered along the way all seemed to sell much
the same wares: rice, occasionally vegetables and fruit, sulphur, gypsum and
divers drugs used in local medical practice. The gypsum was also used to
leaven a bean paste from which bean cheese was made. But, as with most
Chinese food, David could not stomach it. Whenever the chance presented
itself he would buy what in Europe are known as 'mandarin' oranges, with the
thin skin that peeled easily. Sweets and sugar-cane also made an occasional

rare appearance. A new sight for him was that of entirely shaven pigs, cut in two lengthwise, from nose to curly tail, and covered in flies.

At the inn where they stayed one evening the innkeeper showed off his fighting birds. Cock-fighting was a great sport among the Chinese, and good fighting birds commanded prices higher than those paid for good mules. Cocks, quails, and partridges were the birds usually used in this cruel sport. David remembered an incident once when one of the fighting birds had become so furious at the slight whistle from its master that when its cage was opened, instead of profiting from its liberty, it hurled itself at its owner's forehead. Despite all the efforts of the bystanders the bird refused to let go of the screaming man's skin. It took all of David's anatomical and medical skill to get the bird to finally release its hold.

On the last day of the year 1868 they marched 27 miles (43 km). At the end, however, there was difficulty in procuring shelter at the inn in the large walled city of Lungchang. The innkeeper was demanding an

A Szechwan market place.

exorbitant rent, assuming that the foreigner was a man of importance and great wealth. The next day, New Year's Day, they covered more than 33 miles (53 km), passing through endless fields of poppies grown for their rich opium. The men and oxen they passed seemed to be engaged in transporting coal, a very necessary commodity for the bitterly cold winters.

A loud scream rent the air and before David knew what was happening a lunatic, his hands behind his back, rushed past. Poor fellow, David thought, he must have just escaped from the lunatic asylum, if they have such an institution in the village. Everyone turned to stare at the poor fellow.

147

Cock-fighting was a popular pastime in China. Cocks, quails, and partridges were used in this sport.

'Move out,' the stunned onlookers shouted as the lunatic, having turned, bore down on them. As he went past, David saw that his hands were not tied behind his back: he was trying to soothe his sizzling backside. Everyone burst out laughing. It was common practice for people to carry under their garments small baskets containing jars filled with live coals, to provide warmth in the bitter cold. The baskets were attached to their backs by their trouser belts. This poor fellow's jar had broken, resulting in his roasted backside!

Leaving Lungchang the condition of the road deteriorated alarmingly; it was narrow and slippery, with little or no paving-stones. It was very crowded, and the many ponies and oxen held up their progress. Extra care had to be taken of the couriers, who trotted their ponies at a half-gallop with complete disregard for anyone who was in their way. Sugar-cane fields replaced the poppy fields. At Pei-mu-chen David was glad to be able to buy sugar, though unrefined, to sweeten his diet of rice and water.

At the inner gate of Chengtu, the provincial capital, David was detained for a long period while his papers were scrutinised. He was very annoyed with the French Embassy in Peking that had given him a passport in which the chief mandarin interpreter had deliberately left out a formality which rendered the document invalid and useless. To think that he had travelled all those many thousands of miles without anyone spotting the error, till he reached this remote outpost of the Empire. The soldiers could not understand why he should be transporting so many plant and animal specimens. David had added a lot of new specimens to his natural history collection on this fairly short excursion: a new species of forsythia with large flowers but no fragrance, seeds of tallow and alder trees, cottony seeds of an anemone with beautiful violet flowers, etc. In the end he resorted to the age-old remedy to get out of his dilemma — a bribe which was gratefully accepted.

On his way to the residence of Monseigneur Pinchon, the apostolic vicar of North Szechwan, David chanced to pass through the market.

His eyes popped at the large variety of birds for sale – golden pheasants, collarless pheasants, and pigeons with large collars, parrots from south-western Tibet, some with red beaks, others with black beaks. He offered to buy an adult male lophophorus from a Chinaman taking it as a present to a mandarin. The bird had been caught in Tibet. But the judicious Chinaman decided it would be a wiser long-term policy to retain the mandarin's favour than to accept any immediate cash benefit.

The fact that David's boxes, with much of his collecting equipment, had not yet arrived by river from Chungking, and would not be arriving for another twenty days or so, decided him to postpone his start for the College at Muping, which he intended to use as a base for his explorations. In the intervening time he decided to make a short excursion to Ho-pa-ch'ang, where there was a small college, in the high mountains north of Chengtu.

Chinese customs guards, similar to those who detained David at Chengtu.

The route traversed a region frequented by marauding bands of brigands. David was advised to postpone his journey till after the Chinese New Year. There would be less snow on the mountains then. But, as David recorded in his diary that evening,

> If I am to be held back by fears of this kind I shall never do any exploring since the wild places, reputed to be the haunts of thieves and murderers, are precisely the ones that offer the most in the way of natural history in China. For safety only and to assuage evil intentions I shall make sure to keep my gu much in evidence.

On 15 January 1869, David set off in single file with Ouang Thomè and four porters northwards across the plain of Chengtu. On the way they passed many streams of clear water, carefully restrained by bags of pebbles, made of braided bamboo. The streams turned many mills with horizontal wheels, above which were built bamboo and wood houses, the walls and roofs made of thatch. During the day they crossed several streams on fine wooden bridges covered with roofs, resembling Chinese houses. One of these 'house-bridges' was over 260 paces long. Merchants had set out their wares: sweets, sugar-cane, sugar from fermented meal, sweet potatoes, rolls of unleavened bread, etc.

By the afternoon they were in the midst of high, steep, partially wooded mountains, cultivated here and there, their summits draped in fog. This was the classic land of the bandits he had heard so much about but for once he was left in peace; the robbers evidently had no use for such paltry pickings.

At the college David was told about a famous hunter who lived about 10 miles (16 km) further north, still higher in the mountains. David decided to visit him.

Mr Ho, the hunter, came out to greet David, and introduced him to the very simple but charming family. The old man of the house, the grandfather, was an octogenarian, yet still vigorous and robust, and looked not more than sixty. In his day he, too, had been a great hunter. He complained that much of the forests had been destroyed, but there still remained much for the keen hunter – pheasants of several varieties, wild boars, two kinds of forest ante-lopes, two species of muntjac, and the valuable musk-deer. On the wall behind the handsome old man were the hides of a large antelope and a badger that were unknown to David. David was surprised to find a chapel in the house. When the visiting priest made his rounds, the Christians in the vicinity assembled at Mr Ho's house.

The house was in a most picturesque setting, surrounded by magnificent conifers, such as the *Keteleeria*, with trunks rising to a great height before branching out, crowned with a dark green pyramidal top. In the garden were rows of magnolia with very large deciduous leaves. The magnolia was prized for its bark which was used in the preparation of a very expensive medicine called *Lo-po*. David recognised the fragrant camphor trees, called *Lsiang-chao-mu*, which furnished the wood called rosewood. In the market at Chengtu David had seen pretty boxes and caskets made of this fragrant camphor wood. Through the floorboards of his room David could see the clear stream bubbling and babbling into the valley below.

Next day David, dressed like the mountaineers of the valley and wearing sandals of flattened bamboo and heavy wool stockings, set off with Ho and his dogs. Often the forests and thickets became impenetrable because of the vines and brambles; they had to use a hatchet to hack their way through. They followed the tracks of a musk-deer, but soon lost the trail in the snow and ice.

Quails fighting.

The musk-deer was much prized by the local people because the pods which the male musk-deer carries in a pouch under the skin of its abdomen was the source of the highly scented and valuable musk. The hollow, extremely rough, hair of the musk-deer was used for stuffing cushions and mattresses. There was a brisk commerce in musk in these regions, as there was in the skins of wild animals, rhubarb, turquoises and gold-dust.

The hunters followed the tracks of a *gaélu* (wild ass), clearly visible in the snow, but met with no success.

Early one morning David was woken by the sound of much shouting and wailing. Evidently bandits had descended upon the house of one of Mr Ho's neighbours and, after pillaging everything, had burnt the house down. The unfortunate family had come to inform Mr Ho, who was the equivalent of mayor or headman of the district, much loved and respected by his fellow Christians and by non-Christians alike. He was a man of action, firm and just. In no time at all he had mobilised a group of fifty men, armed with guns, who set off with their dogs in pursuit of the robbers. The footprints in the snow led the group to the gang, who were soon overtaken and justice summarily exacted. The unfortunate family recovered most of their belongings. The

151

robbers were obviously new to the region and did not know of Mr Ho, otherwise they would have thought twice before making an attack within his jurisdiction.

David had now been away from Chengtu for about a month; his baggage would have arrived by now. He decided to return to Chengtu. Besides, his excursion had been very successful: in addition to encountering the musk goat*, he had found two new species of wild sheep. He had been able to identify fifteen species of goat, many of which were unknown before, and had seen several antelopes. Indeed, of the four antelopes native to China, David had discovered three. One of these was the takin (*Budorcas taxicolor*), a large and fierce animal, feared by the local inhabitants as much as the tiger. Another antelope David found in the high forests was the *Naemorhedus davidiana* (here he forewent his accustomed modesty to attach his name to one of his discoveries). The third antelope that he had discovered was the *Naemorhedus candatus*, which closely resembled the chamois of the Alps. He had collected over fifty-five specimens of birds. One of these was the very curious *lao-chang-tze* (old gentleman who climbs), so called because of its habit of climbing to the top of shrubs.

Before leaving Mr Ho David tried to recompense him and his family for all the hospitality they had bestowed on him, but they were adamant in their refusal of any present or cash.

At Chengtu David met again Fathers Bompas and Pellé, who had brought his trunks by way of river from Chungking. His equipment having arrived, he could now begin his long exploration of the mountains of Muping. There was yet one more circumstance to delay his travel plan, however – the Chinese New Year! During the New Year festivities no one worked or travelled, and all inns were closed. The Chinese New Year, the most important holiday through-out the Empire, was on 11 February. On this day everyone, dressed in their best clothes, consisting of a long silk dress, visits relatives, supervisors and friends; no one omits this polite duty. The visitor carries his gift with much ostenta-tion and pomp. Good manners demand that supervisors accept only a part of the gift.

For the next several days the celebrations were in full swing. From all sides the closed shops resounded to the frightful noises of tom-toms and other percussion instruments, while their proprietors made up for their customary parsimony with luxurious entertainment. Almost all their year's savings would be spent on these festivities.

---

*Zoologists today acknowledge no such animal. Could David have been wrong in his identification? Or could this be yet another animal which has become extinct in the last century?

14

MUPING:
THE PROMISED LAND

On 22 February 1869 David set off from Chengtu for the independent principality of Muping, 'the promised land where everyone has said there are marvels'. The diary adds: 'I admit, however, that I am not over-enthusiastic, remembering the number of times I have been misled by Chinese promises'. David planned to spend one year in Muping, studying and collecting plant and animal specimens. He was accompanied by Ouang Thomè and four porters. He was always amazed at the strength of these men: of ordinary physique, brought up on very meagre and almost entirely vegetarian diets, often ill with lung diseases, and yet capable of carrying loads of up to 170 pounds (77 kg) on their backs. They would cover 30 miles (48 km) a day as a matter of course.

They set off across the seemingly endless plains of Chengtu, passing mile after mile of rice-fields. Houses, when one came upon them, were hidden under clumps of bamboo and trees; patches of broad beans and mustard broke up the monotony of rice. It was a fine day to start any expedition, the lilting song of the mandarin blackbirds adding to the joy. White herons fed lazily in the small rivers and streams.

On these vast plains the people of Szechwan had resisted the incursions of the present Manchu dynasty of Imperial China. But the Chinese warlords had been too strong and the local people not only defeated, but almost exterminated. The population had been replaced by immigrants from neighbouring lands. Remnants of the original race could still be recognised: they were taller and less yellow than the Chinese, the men had more of a beard, and their eyes and hair were of a more chestnut or auburn hue.

Occasionally the heavily laden porters would halt, but they would not untie or unload the baggage from their shoulders. They would merely sit back on a stick, as on a shooting-stick, with the load resting against a tree-trunk or bank of earth, when these could be found. On one occasion they stopped not from tiredness, but at the strange sight of twelve tiny dwarfs heading for

On the occasions when the heavily laden porters halted, they did not put down their loads, but merely sat on a stick which resembled a shooting-stick.

Chengtu. These were the first dwarfs David had seen in China: how strange, where the population was of generally good physique and the average man was tall! That day they covered 26 miles (42 km) westward of Chengtu.

As it was still the Chinese New Year, it was difficult to find an inn that would open to them. Finally, they were able to tempt one wretched innkeeper to offer them a dirty, damp, tiny room, into which they all squeezed. Before going to sleep the porters all dipped their feet into hot water. David, too, took off his light sandals made of cords of beaten bamboo, which he found very comfortable for walking on snow and in the mountains, and did likewise. This was a hygienic precaution that the mountain porters adhered to rigidly. They lay down on the bare earth, one next to the other, but the fleas and the smell made sure that there was little sleep for David.

Next morning, David put on his sandals by winding the long pieces of cotton cloth round his ankles and calves. This was done as a protection against rheumatism by the local people. He put the blue turban on his head and pulled on the wide, short, fluttering trousers. He was dressed in the fashion of the people of western Szechwan so as to be as inconspicuous as possible.

They continued their march westward; in the distance they could see the high mountains of Tibet. On the way he was able to capture a large civet cat, as big as a dog but with shorter legs and striking black and white markings on its back. Once they passed several men carrying ingots of lead from a nearby silver mine. Once, too, he had proof of the hardness of heart and lack of compassion of the Chinese: a beggar, naked except for a few rags, lay prostrate in a ditch, his only belongings the wooden staff, on which he had staggered from village to village, and a bundle. While the poor wretch breathed his last, men and women laughed and joked around the dying man. Some philanthropist with a misplaced sense of charity had placed an open coffin next to him.

After a week of journeying the plains gave way to the forested hills and mountains of Tibet – the haunt of tigers and robbers. The peoples of the region, called Man-tzu, which means barbarian, had a reputation for evil that was acclaimed throughout the Empire. They were strong

An inn at a village on the border between Szechwan and eastern Tibet.

and brave people but fearful rogues always armed with long swords and knives which they never hesitated to use at the slightest provocation. David learnt that some months earlier two of these Man-tzu had met two other fighters near Kiunglai. A quarrel had ensued and they had lashed at each other with such ferocity with their swords that all four combatants fell dead. Even the women of Man-tzu carried arms.

On the path they passed a famous spring, strewn with rounded boulders and pebbles gathered by the local people to use in their pillows, the stones being very cool in summer. That afternoon they reached the last Chinese village, Ta-hung-miao (the large red pagoda). The incessant rain impeded their progress: that evening they were not able to reach their scheduled halting-place. They spent the night in what passed for a miserable little inn, open to all the winds. In the centre of the room was a small vessel of glazed earth in which burnt a few argols. But these produced more smoke than heat. In the ceiling was a hole to let the smoke out, but all it did was let in the snow and rain. The only food the inn could supply was corn in the form of round cakes, baked in the cinders of the fire. With them went butter, veined with dark green, like gorgonzola, but when David saw that it was lined with a liberal admixture of hairs, both yak and human, he stuck to the dry corn.

While his porters, laden as they were, took a less difficult route, David and Thomé set off on a more direct one, though this involved climbing and then descending a very high and steep mountain. The *la*, or pass, leading through the mountain was at a height of 10,500 feet (3,200 m). The tall, thickly wooded crest formed the border between the province of Szechwan in China and the principality of Man-tzu in Muping. Far in the distance a gleaming white river snaked its way down from the eternal snows to lose itself in the vast plains of China.

The tall cryptomeria trees reminded him of the firs of his native France. On their way they passed a Tibetan woman riding a donkey, a baby fastened to her shoulders by large leather straps. Behind her was a pack-horse she was leading by a long chord; two basket panniers hung symmetrically from its well-laden back, from each of which a pink-faced cherub peered out with saucer eyes at the strange white foreigner. At the rear came a surly red-haired dog with squinting eyes. David could not get over the face of the Tibetan woman: it was blackened with a varnish that made her look hideous. The custom dated back 200 years. Nomekhan (Nomun-Khan), a pious lama king, was alarmed at the immorality then rife in his country, an immorality that had even penetrated the lamaseries. The men were unable to resist the advances of women, who were competing with each other in beautifying themselves. The lama king decided to put an end to this dissoluteness, and women were ordered to make themselves as ugly as possible before stepping out. The women who daubed their faces most disgustingly were considered the most pious. This custom was still observed, but only in regions subject to the Dalai Lama.

The detour proved well worth their while. Despite the difficulties and dangers of the journey David was able to note at least fifteen species of rhododendron, some so large that their trunks exceeded 1 foot (0·3 m) in diameter. Among the pines he spotted a conifer with leaves like those of the American Sequoia. Trunks of large *Sha-mu* (pine), which had been felled by order of the prince of Muping, to erect a barrier against the invading Chinese troops, lay rotting on the ground. Footprints of pheasants and tragopans (horned pheasants) could be seen in the snow, but the birds eluded David.

1 March 1869 was David's first day in Muping. The principality was one of numerous small barbarian states into which the vast territory between China, Tibet and Mongolia was divided. The region was a veritable congeries of different nationalities, languages and religions. There were the Tibetans, with their black eyes, beards, small, contracted eyes, high cheekbones, pug noses, wide mouths and thin lips. They had fair skin; the upper classes as white as Europeans, which enabled David to avoid standing out as too obviously a foreigner. They were of medium height and combined the agility and suppleness of the Chinese with the force and vigour of the Tartars. They were brave, fearless and very religious, though not as credulous as the Tartars. They lived very frugally, their ordinary repast consisting of buttered tea and *tsamba*, mixed together by finger. Their drink was an acid liquor made from

fermented barley. Cleanliness, however, was not one of their virtues.

There were also the Houng-Mao-Eul, or Long Hairs, who were Tibetans, too. They did not shave their heads but let their hair flow over their shoulders, clipping it occasionally with scissors. They were extremely warlike, and walked proudly, with heads erect, the right arm out of the sleeve and resting on their sabre hilts, with rifles on their backs. Let no man stand in their way.

The Si-Fan, or Eastern Tibetans, were there, also. They, too, were indomitably brave and exceedingly addicted to warfare. The present Dalai Lama was a Si-Fan who had been chosen from a poor and obscure home in the principality of Ming-chen-t'u-ssu. At the time when Fathers Huc and Gabet visited Lhasa the Dalai Lama was only a child of nine; so they had conducted their religious debates with the Regent in the palace of the Buddha-La (Potala). The Si-Fan had the most profound contempt for the Chinese. Like the Tartar-Mongols, the East Tibetans were nomads, passing their lives tending their flocks and herds of sheep, goats and yaks. However, their crouching black tents, which Huc had immortally compared to spiders, could not be compared with the Mongol tents: they were no warmer or more solid than ordinary travelling tents; indeed, they were very cold and fragile, yielding to any strong wind.

Here also lived the Man-tzu, or barbarians. They differed considerably from the Chinese, in appearance and in language resembling the Tibetans, whose Buddhist religion they had adopted. Their clothes were made of coarse wool which they made themselves. The Man-tzu kept yaks, cows, goats, sheep and some small horses. They grew mainly wheat, maize and buckwheat. Their white, lime-washed houses were built of stone and were often several storeys high, something rare in China proper. They were a simple and honest people, except where they had come in contact with the duplicitous Chinese.

Some years previously no Chinese were to be seen in Muping, but the situation had changed, and the industrious and ubiquitous Chinese were now found throughout the principality, taking possession of the land under one pretext or another.

David made his headquarters at the College in Muping, which had been built fifty years previously by the missionaries when they had had to flee from the religious persecutions in China. Father Dugrité, the young French priest in charge of the College, provided him with a room and also made available a room in the carpentry workshop for his botanical and zoological work. With the help of several Chinese priests Father Dugrité ran the College for just over fifty students. David planned to spend a season at the College exploring the environs of Muping, so he recruited a few experienced hunters to assist him in his explorations.

A Tibetan house: white, lime-washed, made of stone, and often several storeys high.

It was not long before David was engrossed in his scientific work. He was soon classifying the various species of leopard to be found in the mountains. The local hunters captured these animals by poisoning them with centipedes and tiger beetles. He added a Scops owl (the small horned owl) with a red iris, and a tawny owl, to his rapidly growing collection. He was delighted with a fine specimen of *Tragopan temminckii* (pheasant), and one of the female Lady Amherst pheasant, that some of his hunters brought him. The wildcat they provided also represented a new species.

Little did David know at the time that that day, 11 March 1869, was to be a red-letter day in the annals of exploration. He and a few of his hunters were resting on some large felled pines, when a well-dressed man, who was called Li, came upon them. He was the principal landowner in the valley, and he invited them to rest at his home, where he could offer them tea and biscuits.

David stooped under the low doorway which led into a well-furnished room, with stools and rugs and skins. He froze as his eyes fixed on something on the wall opposite. Slowly he walked over to the wall and gently stroked his hand across the skin. His fingers moved from the soft white fur of the skin on to the black eyes and little black ears and black legs. He could hardly believe his eyes. The legendary *pei-hsuing* or *beishung* (white bear) was not a myth; it was true. Its skin was there before his very eyes; he had passed his fingers over its soft inviting fur.

The diary for the day records finding the famous 'white and black bear . . . which will provide an interesting novelty for science'. The hunters promised to capture one for David.

Three days later David's hunters did arrive with an animal but it was not the black and white bear; it was a huge boar with very short ears. Some days later, at an altitude of 8,000 feet (2440 m), while the royal eagles and the common crane circled overhead, David found the fir, *Abies*. Here, too, was the first rhododendron in flower.

An air of foreboding hung over the College. News had arrived that an important mandarin of the Chengtu government had persuaded the princes of

Man-tzu to exterminate all Christians established in their states, and this had recently been done in the district of Yung-yang. No one could be sure if these rumours were true or if they were stories put about by the government to frighten away the missionaries, but the toll of missionaries murdered in recent years had gone up and up. Life for the converts was equally hazardous and difficult.

On 17 March in fine, sunny weather, Ouang Thomè and David left the College at seven in the morning to explore the big mountain of Hongchantin. Armed with guns and natural history equipment, they entered a wild valley of the famous mountain. Little did they know this was so nearly to be their last day on earth. David's diary recounts what happened:

> By following the steep banks of a stream which is still half-frozen we reach, towards 11 o'clock, the foot of a series of noisy and foaming waterfalls where, all of a sudden, the narrow path we had been following came to an end. After eating our dinner, a crust of bread moistened in icy water, we begin climbing the steep slopes which enclose this narrow valley, hoping to find a way around the unwelcoming waterfalls; but it is in vain. For four whole hours we clamber from rock to rock as high as we can, clinging on to trees and roots. Anything which is not vertical is covered with frozen snow. Twenty times our courage fails us to continue this horribly painful ascent. These immense steep slopes would frighten the boldest of people. Fortunately the trees and shrubs prevent us from seeing too clearly the abysses over which we are suspended, sometimes hanging on only by our hands. We continue this exhausting gymnastic ascent for four long hours, often repenting having tried to scale these abominable precipes where we see no trace of the foot of man. But after reaching a certain height it becomes impossible to descend without sliding or slipping on the ice. Already we are worried and our imaginations are stirred when we see in the distance and almost vertically below us the frothing white water of the torrent which bounds noisily from rock to rock, from cascade to cascade. What shall we do? We are badly scratched and our clothes and equipment soaked. Our strength is exhausted and seems to have left us completely as has never happened before. The situation has become serious and we realise it is a question of life or death. The danger is extreme. At one moment we cannot keep our

159

balance on the ice, at another moment we plunge into the half-melted snow, and sometimes the bushes and rocks which we cling on to break or come away and we slide to another tree or neighbouring rock. Fortunately my robust young man is seeing it through better than I would ever have hoped. Twice, however, I hold him back when he is already slipping to the very edge of abysses. He says that if we do not die that day we never will!

A Christian from eastern Tibet.

The unimaginable difficulties of this monkey-like descent absorb so much of our attention that we pay little attention to the still fresh tracks of several large animals in the snow. There is danger here also because there are fierce bears and wild bulls which, it is said, the mountain people fear more than leopards and even tigers. The snow has soaked our ammunition and even filled up the barrels of our rifles. We pay even less attention to the striped squirrels which leap agilely amongst the furry lichens hanging from the branches of age-old pines, or to the yelling nutcrackers which haunt these high forests.

At long last the sun, which has shone till near three o'clock, begins to disappear in the thick fog in which we soon find ourselves lost. Hoping no longer to reach the crest of the mountain where we had thought we might find a pathway which humans could negotiate and being utterly exhausted, we are compelled to descend so as not to be overtaken by night in these dreadfully solitary places. We stop for a while to recover from our fear and exhaustion and to take breath. No noise breaks the silence, apart from the distant sound of waterfalls and the plaintive croaking of the brown carrion crow. I also recognise the muffled lowing of a wild bull, but I am careful not to say anything to my Chinese companion so as not to add to his discouragement and fear. In such situations it is not difficult to pray. We do so with fervour and then give ourselves up to Providence.

We descend the immense wall of over one thousand metres the same way as we climbed it, by going from one tree to another, from one rock to another. Often the sides of the mountain are vertical. Three times we lose traces of our ascent and are forced to climb back to find a mountain ridge along which it will be possible to descend, for all the declivities are so steep, are covered with snow and slippery ice and are bereft of bushes and trees to which one can cling. However, we find two ravines which we are forced to cross horizontally, accompanied by the great danger of being swept down and being dashed into the chasms. Miraculously I hold myself back once from the edge of an abyss and at the same time stop my companion, who has slipped on the ice.

Finally, after an hour and a half of this inhuman descent we arrive at the bottom of the mountain, on the banks of the foaming torrent. Both our clothes and our hands are badly torn; our hunting equipment is in a sorry state. We are soaked with perspiration and water and, despite all the snow we have swallowed, are burning with thirst. But we believe we are safe and thank God for having led us out of the danger.

Unfortunately we are far from coming to the end of our miseries because night is falling and we are still five leagues from our house. Where we are there is not a house, nor cabin, nor human being to be seen. To add to our difficulties the day's heat has melted so much snow on the heights that the streams are greatly swollen. Nevertheless, summoning up what strength and courage remains to us we go forward, armed with long sticks, across the water and mud and rocks which form our appalling path.

But soon the night becomes very dark, and to add to our miseries it begins to rain. There is no choice: we have to keep walking and that is what we do for two hours, along unknown paths where I have been only once before. Finally we can go no farther: it is impossible to continue. It is in vain to grope amongst the rocks or to venture up to our waists into the icy waters of the stream, now a veritable river, because we cannot see anything.

161

The least unpleasant alternative and the only thing to do is to stop there in the first shelter or rocky cave which we manage to feel with our hands despite the hunger, cold, sweat and being completely soaked. In this extreme situation we decide to break our perilous journey, even at the risk of dying of cold and immobility, when all of a sudden we hear human voices. Deo gratias! We have been saved once again.

We shout out with vigour and soon a man comes running up with a lamp and leads us to his cabin. We had not suspected there could be any human habitation in these wild gorges. The kind inhabitants of this little wooden house are very welcoming to us and set about preparing some potatoes and two cakes of maize which we devour with pleasure and gratitude. They are even so good as to want to give us one of their beds, made from branches of a tree; but we thank them and spend the entire night near an enormous fire, busy drying and warming ourselves as much as we can and reciting our daily prayers.

The path consisted of tree trunks resting on wooden pylons which had been driven into the mountainside. The narrow track, just wide enough for a laden pack-horse, wound giddily along the cliff-face.

This day, so full of misadventures, did not yield much for my collections of natural history. A grey squirrel and a 'Nucifraga', both of them new species to me, are the only animals I have been able to take

162

today. These frightful mountains, where we were almost lost, are quite well populated with large mammals; but these are not for me!

Some days later David was exploring again. He stopped as a flight of snow-partridges, alarmed at his approach, swept away into the mist. The road became increasingly precipitous. As he turned a corner of the mountain his heart stopped: the savage beauty of the scenery took one's breath away, so did the narrow path he had to negotiate. The path consisted of tree-trunks resting on wooden pylons which had been driven at an angle into the mountain-side. The low wooden balustrade contributed less to safety than to peace of mind. A boiling torrent writhed milkily under a sheer drop 1,000 feet (300 m) below them. The narrow track, just wide enough for a laden pack-horse, wound giddily along the cliff-face, then went down, and down, to and fro, across the mountain face, till it reached the river.

Back at the College, David was busy preparing the many plant and animal specimens he had collected when there was a knock on his door. An agitated young Chinese seminarian informed David he had a very important visitor in Father Dugrité's office. David wondered who this could be.

The young man, hopelessly overdressed in his military uniform, was very fair. Was he a mercenary in the employ of Governor Wu? David knew some French Army officers who had been in the employ of the Chinese government as instructors of the Imperial Army, who had been dismissed on the pretext that the government had no money to pay them. Could he be one of them?

He was a pompous, arrogant man; David did not warm to his manner. He was abrupt and came to the point straight away. 'You must cease your hunting,' he commanded.

'Oh! And who says that?' asked David.

'I do!'

'But you have no authority here,' David reminded him.

'I am here at the behest of His Excellency the T'u-ssu, the prince. He has forbidden all hunting. You and your hunters must desist forthwith.'

'I suggest you pass that order to the hunters yourself,' replied David, knowing how little notice they would take either of the captain's orders or of the governor's.

'I have warned you. The consequences will be serious.' With that the captain gathered up his sword, and strode out of the room.

David smiled to himself and was still smiling as Father Dugrité entered the room. The priest had been eaves dropping, and was concerned: he did not want to incur the wrath of Governor Wu. Wu was an evil man, who even included his own sister in his harem, and anyone who disobeyed his slightest

Soldiers of the type that came to threaten David and
persuade him to stop his hunting activities.

wish disappeared in the hungry waters of the river. At the last persecution instituted by him several Christians had been murdered by drowning.

Next day David passed on the captain's message to the hunters. They nodded and went away. But the specimens of animals still arrived each day. When David made enquiries they told him that the animals had been found in territory *outside* Governor Wu's jurisdiction, and David was happy to accept an explanation he knew could not possibly be true. He agreed with the hunters: hunting was their livelihood, so why should only the governor have the monopoly?

It was 23 March 1869 that Father David became the first westerner ever to set eyes on a giant panda. His diary records the occasion:

> My Christian hunters returned today after a ten-day absence. They bring me a white bear, which they took alive but unfortunately killed so that it could be carried more easily. The young white bear, which they sell to me very dearly, is all white except for the legs, ears, and around the eyes, which are deep black. The colours are the same as those I saw in the skin of an adult bear the other day at the home of Li, the hunter. This must be a new species of 'Ursus' (bear), very remarkable not only because of its colour, but also for its paws which are hairy underneath, and for other characteristics.

On 1 April the hunters brought David another 'white bear', this time a fully adult one. Its colours were exactly like those of the young 'bear' he had seen earlier, except that the darker parts were less black and the white parts more soiled. It had a very large head, with a short, round snout, unlike the pointed snout of the Peking bear. David appreciated the significance of his discovery, but it would be months before he could let the scientific world in Europe know. The courier from Chengtu was arriving in a day's time. He could send a letter via him to Professor Alfonse Milne-Edwardes, son of the Director of the Natural History Museum in Paris, telling him of his find. That evening he sat down and wrote:

> As it will not be possible for my collection to arrive in Paris for a very long time, I pray you will publish immediately the following description of a bear which seems to me to be new to science.
>
> *Ursus melanoleucus*, A. D. (Armand David, not Anno Domini!) Very large according to my hunters. Ears short. Tail very short. Hair fairly short; beneath the four feet very hairy. Colours: white, with the ears, the surroundings of the eyes, the tip of the tail and the four legs brownish black. The black on the forelegs is joined over the back in a straight band. I have just received a young bear of this kind and I have seen the mutilated skins of adult specimens. The colours are always the same and equally distributed. I have not seen this species, which is easily the prettiest kind of animal I know, in the museums of Europe. Is it possible that it is new to science?

This description of the giant panda appeared in the Bulletin of the Natural History Museum in Paris later that year. A few days later he was able to add a postscript to the letter:

> An adult female of the black and white bear has just come into my possession. The coat is yellowish and the black is darker and shinier than in the young specimen.

The poor courier was taken aback to be so enthusiastically welcomed by a white man. David could hardly wait for his arrival – and was even more enthusiastic for his departure, with his precious missive. Fortunately, couriers seemed to enjoy a charmed existence. Though often carrying money and valuables in addition to letters, they somehow managed to get through regions infested with robbers without ever coming to harm.

David's hunting continued apace; day by day his collection of new

A Himalayan black bear, thought to be related to the giant panda.

species of animals grew. A few days after obtaining the giant panda the hunters brought him a wild boar, striped similarly to the European boar. They also brought him a *chan-tche-cua*, or 'lesser panda'. It was a cuddly little animal, with a voice that resembled a child's, that lived in trees or holes, up in the high mountains. Its food was vegetarian or carnivorous according to what was available. The rock antelope that the hunters brought was also new to David.

On 4 May the hunters who had left a fortnight earlier for the eastern regions returned, bringing with them six monkeys of a new species, quite unknown to western zoologists, which the Chinese called *chin-tsin-hou* or 'golden-brown monkey'. These animals were very robust, with large muscular limbs. Their faces were most unusual: green-blue in colour, with their noses turned up almost to their foreheads. Their tails were long and strong, and their backs covered with silky, golden hair, almost 18 inches (45 cm) in length.

So, the monkey demon, with turquoise face, red and gold body, and nose turned up to its eyes as depicted in Chinese art and folk-lore, was based on a living creature. It was eventually named *Rhinopithecus roxellanae* after Roxellana, a young Russian girl abducted by Turkish raiders in Galicia, in east-central Europe. She was sold as a slave and placed in the harem of the Turkish Sultan Suleiman the Magnificent. She is described as having a face that showed intelligence and pride, with high cheek-bones, a fine pointed chin, immense clear eyes of intense blue, and a small mouth with full lips in the form of a heart. Silky blonde hair, with reflections of russet gold, trailed over her back and

down to her ankles. In 1523 Roxellana – 'the favoured laughing one' –
became the Sultan's wife, a remarkable achievement because Turkish
sultans had not married for hundreds of years. More than four centuries later she captivated the
French zoologist, Alfonse Milne-
Edwardes of the Natural History
museum in Paris. Milne Edwardes
took one look at the monkey David
had sent, with its turquoise face, red
and gold body, and nose turned up.
Yes, it had to be named after Roxellana.

During the Ch'ing Dynasty the
skins of these golden monkeys were
made into capes to be worn only by
the Manchu officials. Such cloaks
were believed to ward off rheumatism. The monkeys have a very practical way of keeping warm in their
snow-covered habitat. They hug
each other, bury their faces in their
long silky hair and then secure each
other fast by twining their long tails
about them.

Animal discoveries were coming thick and fast. David had barely

Some scientists believed that the giant panda
was related to the racoon family. The bone
structure and dental system of the giant
panda distinguishes it from bears and puts it
nearer to racoons and lesser pandas.

finished describing the 'golden-brown' monkeys when he discovered the remarkable Macacus monkey. He named it *Macacus tibetanus*. He then
obtained the skin of a *gaélu*, about the height of a donkey, that is, twice the
height of the *Naemorhedus goral candatus* of Peking. During his three months
at Muping David collected twenty-three species of mammal new to him and to
Western science. He made an equally impressive collection of new birds,
butterflies and insects.

David regretted that his preoccupation with the fauna of the region had
prevented him from doing full justice to the botany of the area. Even so, he sent
back to Europe a remarkable collection of plants quite unknown to the western
world. These included no less than fifteen species of rhododendron; a gentian

167

with pale blue flowers; a large, handsome anemone with bluish-white flowers; a magnificent magnolia with purple flowers; a fine blue aconite; a lily; a rhubarb with palmate leaves, and many more. There was also the plant of the famous *pai-mu*, famous in Chinese *materia medica*: this was a true fritillary with large yellow leaves. Near the borders of the river he had found the sumach, from which the varnish resin is extracted: oblique gashes were made into the trunks of the trees, and at the lower end of the gash a mollusc shell (the clam *Anodonta*) was attached to collect the precious extract. Here he had found that evergreen trees abounded, along with large conifers with hard wood and large leaves resembling sequoia.

'For three weeks now I have been feeling awful. This intestinal irritation has got worse from day to day.'

'Three weeks!' Dugrité said in astonishment. 'Ill for three weeks and you've been doing all this gadding around.' David just nodded: he was too ill to speak any more. He wanted to be left alone. The superior and Ouang left the room quietly.

For a week David just lay there. None of the conventional medicaments proved efficacious, and it was some days before he could even sit up in bed.

'What day is it?' he asked Ouang. Ouang told him. 'The middle of June already! And there is still so much to do.' It was pelting with rain outside. 'How long has it been raining?' he asked Ouang as he gazed out of his room at the pelting rain.

'For almost all the time you have been ill,' Ouang replied. This was some comfort to David; at least he had not lost valuable time. 'All the rivers are swollen,' Ouang went on. 'Most of the bridges made from tree-trunks have been washed away. This morning three unfortunate travellers fell into the water and their bodies were spotted washed up on some rocks. It has not been possible to recover the bodies.'

The days rolled by, the monotony broken only by the roar of landslides which crashed into the valleys below. The clap of rocks bouncing off one another could be heard. As his strength returned slowly, so did David's desire to press on with his collecting. He persuaded himself and the disapproving superior that some physical exercise might speed his recovery, and set off with Ouang to make a whole day's excursion to the distant valley of Thang. He was surprised to come across a lone woman riding a yak, a toothless grin emanating from a wizened witch-like face under a large white hat shaped like a saucepan. He wondered where she came from. A little later a family passed them; the man grinned darkly from under a fox-fur hat. He led two donkeys while his children, in gaudy little bonnets and lashed on to the loads, nodded drowsily to the stride of the animals. His wife, dressed in what looked like a Tibetan carpet, followed on a shaggy Tibetan pony.

The two travellers crossed a roofed and brightly painted bridge over dark green waters swirling 200 feet (61 m) below. They watched a team of yaks bluntly plough through the torrent, like tugs, while the ponies foundered with an air of helplessness among the submerged rocks. David wished he could join the animals in the water: he was feeling terribly hot. In fact he was burning – with fever. Later that day the seminarians rushed to the College gate to help Ouang, who was struggling to hold David up. On entering the College David collapsed. They carried him to his room; he was in a faint for a long time.

He spent another three days and nights of hell, his high fever now cause for alarm. 'If I can get a diuretic I might improve,' he told Father Dugrité. But there was no such medicine around. Instead the seminarians pulled up bamboo roots and boiled them in water as a substitute for 'quack' grass, but the quack remedy proved as ineffectual as the other 'medicines' he had tried. In desperation they gave him goosefoot grass (*Chenopodium album*), which grew wild in the garden, mixed with oil and vinegar. This time the 'medicine' improved matters. For the rest of his stay in Muping David took goosefoot grass as his only nourishment each day.

David was becoming alarmed

David had barely recovered from a severe form of bone typhus than he was again collecting rare plants and animals. This was despite fever and swollen legs, and despite the forbidding and inhospitable terrain.

169

at the state of his animal skins and his insect and plant collections. The extreme humidity was causing the skins to decompose rapidly: his collections were getting covered with mould. Even though it was midsummer and almost tropical heat he kept a fire going in his room to preserve his specimens. Despite the arsenic, salt and alum David used in preparing his specimens, the numerous *dermestes* continued to ravage them: it was essential to preserve the specimens in cabinets. But, as he reported, 'this cannot be done for lack of a good carpenter and of wood. Even the nails must be brought from several days' journey away.'

On 19 July it was the feast day of St Vincent, the man who had founded David's own Order, the Congregation of the Missions. He allowed himself a day off and celebrated with chicken and coffee, even though he had ground the coffee two years previously, which meant that it had lost much of its goodness.

One specimen still eluded David – the bird lophophorus. He was determined to get one, even if it killed him, and he had sought this bird as the lover in the Chinese fairy story had relentlessly gone after the fabulous blue rose, inquiring tirelessly at every source for information. 'That's right! It will kill you,' said Father Dugrité, trying to persuade David out of his mad plan, so soon after his illness.

The 'mad' explorer set off for the black and green schist mountain of Hung-shan-ting, with its sharp crests pointing almost vertically into the sky. 'The paths we take climbing the mountain cause trembling and vertigo. Hunters often lose their lives here.' He was soon above 12,000 feet (3,650 m).

One of the hunters held David back by the arm. 'Listen,' he said.

David listened. It was the whistling call of the elusive lophophorus. But, startled by their approach, it flew away. Out in the open the faintest sounds travel far, and once on the wing the lophophorus flew too quickly and too far to be caught. Just then luck came to David's aid. An immense cloud covered him at the moment when a large lophophorus left the opposite peak. As it unsuspectingly winged in towards them, David was able to bag it. His 'mad' plan had succeeded. What a handsome specimen this *Lophophorus lhuysii* was, a gorgeous pheasant with iridescent green plumage. Another magnificent specimen obtained was the *Crossoptilon coerulescens*, a bird with slate-blue plumage, a red bill, red feet, and a black, velvety head plumage separated from a slate-coloured back by a tiny white band. The tips of its tail-feathers were an iridescent glossy black and the lateral plumes were white.

David was on the mountain again the next day. He was a fiend for punishment for, as he records,

The ascent of Hung-shan-ting is the most laborious imaginable whether because of the distance that has to be traversed in one day or because of the steepness and practical impassability of the paths, always wet, muddy, and sometimes close to frightening abysses. I repeat, one has to be accustomed to dangers so as not to tremble and lose one's equilibrium in some of the crossings, the mere recollection of which makes me shiver.

He watched three elegant musk-deer tiptoe along a narrow edge of rock separating two terrific precipices, searching for their rhododendrons. He was in the rarefied atmosphere of a height of more than 15,000 feet (4,570 m). His companions complained of intense headaches, but David felt no particular discomfort. He recorded the beauty of the scene before him:

At our feet is an immense white sea of fog that extends to the distant horizon. The summits of high mountains rise out of it like islands in an ocean. To the south-west, the principal peaks seem very high. The part we see above the clouds is covered with a great deal of snow. The mountains we see appear twice as high (and perhaps more) as we are, judging by the horizontal lines of immobile clouds. So we are facing peaks comparable to the highest in the Himalayas, and I do not exaggerate in attributing 26,000 – 29,000 feet (7,900 – 8,840 m) to the mountains of eastern Tibet. I am sorry I am not able to give them a name, since the men only know them under the generic name of *Ta-hsiieh-shan* (Large Snowy Mountains).

David was looking out upon the vast Everest range.

High up in these slopes he found three species of rhododendron that he had never seen before. He carefully picked a large number of young plants of each species, especially those with rounded leaves and large, pelargonium-like flowers.

On getting back to the College David learned that the bishop would be sending his couriers to Hankow early in October. This would give him the opportunity to send off his valuable collections of animals and plants with them. He decide to return to Chengtu. First, proper chests had to be made for his specimens; David set to and with his own hands made the makeshift crates, of which he needed three to carry all his specimens. Then came the problem of finding men to carry the chests. Finally, at the end of August David set off on the five-day march to Chengtu, even though he was not well, suffering severe headaches, fever and, more alarmingly, symptoms of typhus. When he finally reached Chengtu, his left foot was swollen and along with the rest of the leg was causing him unbearable pain. He was just about able to crawl into his bed, and his condition grew steadily worse. He became unable to move without the most excruciating pain. The local Chinese physician was summoned.

David listened expectantly as the doctor announced his diagnosis of the illness: 'bone typhus'. He recommended poultices of ginger and onions, soaked with brandy. This was done, while David was confined to bed for twelve days. Slowly the pains eased enough for him to return to Muping, to continue his scientific work, but this time he allowed himself to be carried in a sedan chair for much of the way.

It had been David's hope, health and time permitting, to visit Lungan, a corner of the Chinese Empire bordering on the famous Koko Nor, the largest lake in China. But this hope was not to be realised: David's health had gone. The diary for 11 October reads:

> I have severe pain in my legs and fear the return of my illness of a month ago. The pains in my right leg are so violent that at night they cause me to faint, as I did at Chengtu. The Chinese doctor Lo says the fat of a leopard can lessen my pains.

He could barely walk the few paces to the lavatory let alone hunt for leopards! The next day's diary records:

> I am unable to get up for Mass ... I mind the suffering less than the loss of time caused by my illness. I am very much afraid I cannot carry out my projected journey to Ta-wei, which I wanted so much to visit in person before finally leaving the province of Muping.

Some days later he reported: 'No improvement in my condition, which is complicated by retention of urine ... Although it is Sunday I cannot rise from my bed to celebrate Mass.'

By the end of October his condition was somewhat better. He again set to making five large chests to hold the rest of his collections and skins, and early in November he was strong enough to go climbing again. By imitating the shrill cries of some medium-sized birds (*Paradoxornis*) by whistling he was able to attract some of them near enough for him to catch three.

By now heavy snow was covering the passes. If he was to begin his homeward journey he must start soon. Again he was faced with the problem of finding porters for his five crates of natural history specimens on the eight-day journey to Chengtu. There was much political instability in the region and real fear of war was a major deterrent. However, he had a stroke of good fortune: a group of porters had recently come from Szechwan, carrying sacks of rice. Instead of returning empty-handed they were only too pleased – despite the serious threat to their lives – to return home, receiving an exorbitant bonus to boot. On 22 November 1869 Father David finally began the journey back to Chengtu.

On the return trip down the Yangtze David had to endure all the dangers and inconveniences that he had undergone on his first trip up the mighty Blue River. At Shanghai, however, he was able to send off his valuable collection of plants and animals to Milne-Edwardes, the Director of the Natural History Museum in Paris. From Shanghai David headed out to the Yellow Sea. On 25 July 1870, eight months after he had begun his return trip he reached Chefoo in the Shantung peninsula.

David breathed a sigh of relief as the boat skirted the islands of Miao Tao and entered the calmer waters of the bay of Yen-t'ai. He had paid enough tribute to navigation with his bouts of *mal de mer*. On the left lay Chefoo, nestling neatly on the gentle slopes which gradually rose to medium-high mountains in the distance. Gulls, cormorants and oyster-catchers winged to and fro.

He was pleased to meet Mr Viguier again, a young Parisian, who was a commissioner of customs. They exchanged their items of news. Mr Viguier had found some gold-bearing quartz in a mine not too far away. David, for his part, related some of his adventures and described some of the exotic plants and animals he had discovered. But he was tired. Only one more sea journey and he would be home again, on terra firma. He was looking forward to his rendevous with his colleagues in Tientsin – Father Chévrier and Father Wang, and the good Sisters of Charity.

'What's the matter?' David asked, as he looked anxiously at the young Frenchman. Mr Viguier's face was ashen grey; his mouth open. He made no reply. Had he had a 'turn'? David wondered. He repeated his question.

'Tientsin?' the young man managed to blurt out. 'Haven't you heard?' David frowned as he shook his head. 'The rebels were there. All the mission houses were burnt. All the priests and nuns were massacred. Many Christians too.'

The elusive pheasant *Lophophorus lhuysii* that David had searched
for tirelessly just as the lover in the Chinese fairy story
had relentlessly pursued the fabulous blue rose.

15

GENOA, PARIS AND VERSAILLES

David was up early as usual. He held the rails to steady himself against the ship's rolling, relieved to sense the pitching and tossing lessen perceptibly as the minutes went by. He could now pick out the buildings of the port quite easily. Marseilles. The grip on the rails tightened: he would be home soon. It was the end of 1870. The total destruction of the Vincentian mission at Tientsin had been a bitter blow to him and, coupled with his rapidly deteriorating health, had prompted the authorities to send him back to France to recuperate.

As he was so near Savona he crossed over to Italy to renew acquaintance with friends and colleagues at the College where he had taught prior to going to China. The border guard shook his head without even bothering to look at David's papers. No, he could not enter France.

'But I'm a Frenchman. France is my home. Here, see my papers.' The guard was adamant. There was a war on, the border was closed and that was that.

So David was trapped in Italy, because of a war, the Franco-Prussian War, taking place miles away. He might just as well have stayed in China! But he was not one to bemoan his enforced imprisonment in a foreign country. He went to Genoa, where he was able to catch up with all the latest developments in science, through the journals and the scientists that met regularly at the Museo Civico. Darwin's *Origin of Species* had appeared a few years earlier and his views were the sensation of the time. David himself had thought much about the origin of species, and in his explorations he had been constantly on the look-out for fossils. In his excavations in the diluvial cliffs around Erh-shih-san-hao – where he had picked up his guide, Sambdatchiemda – David had found two large fossil bones: one he classified as the fragment of an elephant's head, the other the end of the lower jaw of a large pachyderm. He had also unearthed prehistoric fragments of old pottery, metal tools and arrowheads made of chalcedony and other hard stones. Near Chungking, where the limestone rocks had metamorphosed into marble, he had found many remnants of shells.

David appreciated how the seemingly most trivial fact could often assume considerable significance in unravelling the mysteries of life and nature. As he wrote in his third diary:

> The smallest facts about nature, provided they are exact, are of great importance today in helping to understand the scheme of the world ... It is of utmost importance that the different forms in which life is manifested be known in order to understand the past. It is necessary to know the distribution of animals and plants over the earth's surface and its waters to understand geological changes which preceded the present epoch ... The study of spiders alone proved that Italy had touched the continent of Africa in ancient times. The examination of mammals, birds, and insects showed Mr Wallace that the three large islands of Malaysia were part of the Asiatic continent, while Celebes, though far from Borneo, was separate, at least back into ancient times, if not always ... The most minute objects, the most insignificant details, are important. A dot, a comma, a small line are not important in themselves but have value in relation to the whole, and can change radically its final significance.

David saw no conflict between evolution and religion. His own views on the origin of species were very much the same as Darwin's. He wrote:

> Is it not reasonable to believe that the principal types of animals and plants have appeared on the earth when and how it pleased God (something that will always be a mystery to man), that they underwent slow modifications and were gradually divided into races, species, and varieties which continued to propagate and increase around the place of their origin?

David was somewhat nonplussed by all the fuss surrounding Darwin's publication. Many of his co-religionists feared that somehow their most cherished beliefs had been upended. The materialists, for whom believing there is *no* God was just as much an act of faith as believing in God, rejoiced as though Darwin had disproved the notion of God, which he had not. It was Darwin who wrote in his *Origin of Species*:

176

> I see no good reason why the views given in this volume should
> shock the religious feelings of any one ... It is just as noble a
> conception of Deity to believe He created a few original forms
> capable of self-development into other and needful forms, as to
> believe he required a fresh act of creation to supply the voids
> caused by the action of His law.

Newton and Laplace had showed how the solar system could function without
daily divine intervention; Darwin and Wallace had done the same thing for
living nature. The ultimate need of God was not repudiated in either case.
Evolution does not explain creation; it merely throws light on the immediate
means by which a wonderful pattern has been (and is being) woven from raw
materials already created. For David, a creation continually developed by
evolution was no less admirable or mysterious than the seven days' wonder of
creation described in Genesis; and it offered just as much scope for religious
reverence. To him the foresight of God which made continuous miraculous
intervention unnecessary was just as wonderful as any miracle. To quote from
Darwin again:

> There is grandeur in this view of life, with its several powers,
> having been originally breathed by the Creator into a few forms
> or into one, and that whilst this planet has gone circling on –
> according to the fixed laws of gravity, from so simple a begin-
> ning endless forms most beautiful and most wonderful have
> been, and are being evolved.

For David, too, life on earth had evolved from simple to complex, but as to how
and why it really happened, he had not the slightest idea. It would simply
remain God's secret. Evolution began only on the second day of creation – with
the elements that are to combine and evolve already created. For David the
first day of creation was the crux of the matter, and there could be no
opposition between science and religion. Science offers no explanation for the
existence of the universe: it cannot explain why there is a universe at all. As
Newton had pointed out: 'first causes are not for science'. Scientific laws and
formulas can be devised which account for the characteristics and behaviour of
objects but it cannot explain *why* the laws hold good. Even if man understood
and could explain everything there would still be need of God. Knowing how
the universe is sustained is not the same as sustaining it.

Newton, Copernicus, Galileo, Descartes, Leibniz, Laplace, Pascal and
Faraday had all been devout practising Christians. Indeed, one of the first
scientists of continental Europe to accept Newton's gravitational theory was

the astronomer and physicist Boscovich, a Jesuit priest. Clavius, Kircher and Secchi, all eminent scientists, were also Jesuit priests. For all of them there was no dichotomy between science and religion; both were the most compelling forces in their lives – as, indeed, they were in David's. Creation, nature and man – these were not what God did or does, but what He is.

Paris surrendered to the besieging forces of Bismarck in January 1871 and the war was over. At last David was able to return to the Mother House of his Order in the rue de Sèvres. He was pleased to hear that the collection of plants and animals that he had sent to the Natural History Museum had not been damaged.

One of David's first acts on reaching Paris was to see the French President himself. He was very aggrieved at the murders of so many of his colleagues, and of priests and nuns of other orders; at the constant harassment and humiliation that missionaries had to suffer in China; at the mandarins deliberately writing out false, invalid papers, with the French authorities seemingly doing very little about it. He would demand that the President see to it that more protection and consideration be given to missionaries.

'He wants to see the President himself,' the bishop's secretary said to his lordship. They both smiled. An ordinary priest to see the President! Indeed! Even the Cardinal would have difficulty in seeing the President these days! David realised there was just as much bureaucracy and red tape in the capital of France as in the capital of China.

For some months the top scientists of Paris had worked on classifying the hundreds of plant and animal specimens that David had shipped from China. He was now there himself and so was able to help Émile Blanchard, the professor at the Jardin des Plantes, with the enormous collection of plants, David Oustalet with the birds of every conceivable hue and colour, size and shape, and Charles Oberthuer with the myriads of insects. The Milne-Edwardes, father and son, had worked on the mammals.

There was such a variety; where did one begin? Of the mammals alone there were numerous different, unique species. The classification of the giant panda posed several problems: was it a bear or some other species of animal? Its size and form resembled those of a bear, especially the Himalayan black bear, which even had a white crescent on its chest. Not only did the giant panda look like a bear; it walked, sat and stood on its hind legs like a bear, which led David to think that the *pei-hsuing* or *beishung* (the 'white bear') was a new species of bear. But there were some striking differences between the giant panda and the bear. A bear can walk on its hindlegs, a giant panda cannot; a giant panda has a special 'thumb' on its forefeet enabling the giant panda to grasp objects, such as bamboo shoots, almost in the manner of humans, while a bear does not. A giant panda has hair on the soles of its feet preventing it from slipping on ice and snow, a bear does not. The giant panda does not hibernate as the bear does, and any self-respecting meat-eating bear would turn up its nose at the giant panda's diet of bamboo (although David did point out that the panda 'does not refuse flesh when the occasion presents itself'.) Another smaller difference is that whilst bears roar, giant pandas bleat, or give out a kind of yodelling cry.

David had sent to Paris not only the skins but also the skull of the giant panda which the hunters had killed in Muping. From his anatomical study of this giant panda, Alfonse Milne-Edwardes concluded that the giant bear was not a bear but rather belonged to a new species. As he reported:

> In its external form the animal very much resembles a bear,
> but its bone structure and dental system clearly distinguish it
> from the bears and puts it nearer to pandas and racoons. It must
> constitute a new genus which I have called 'Ailuropoda'.

This name was chosen to recall the resemblance between the feet of the newly discovered animal and those of Ailurus, the red or lesser panda, the only animal known as a panda in those days. The full scientific name of the giant panda became *Ailuropoda melanoleucus*, 'the panda-like black and white animal'.

It was difficult to imagine the giant panda as a member of the racoon family. The racoon and 'lesser' pandas are much smaller than the giant panda, being about the size of civet cats, and they have a red back and long, bushy, ringed tails. In fact, half the length of the lesser panda consists of tail; whereas the giant panda has a very short tail. But the lesser panda does resemble the giant panda in its black eye-patches and short black legs. Even in modern times zoologists argue as to the correct family of mammals to which the giant panda belongs. The zoologists at the Smithsonian Institute in America, using genetic and molecular techniques (DNA hybridisation) believe that the giant panda and the racoon-like lesser panda should be classified in separate families. Research currently being carried out at the Wolong Nature Reserve in Central China inclines to the view that David held, namely, that the giant panda belongs to the bear family.

In the summer of 1871 an exhibition was held of the plants and animals David had discovered. It drew huge crowds.

David allowed himself a smile as he rode down the rue Morgue, past the museum. The huge billboard looking down on him still proclaimed '*exposition de merveilleux spécimens de plantes et animaux découverts par le célèbre explorateur et savant, le Père Armand David*'. He was celebrated now. That was why he was on his way to Versailles – to meet the President of France. At the palace David expressed his anger and annoyance at how little the French government appeared to be doing to protect its citizens abroad. The President promised he would do all in his power to provide greater protection for missionaries working in countries with which France had treaties. David was no 'ordinary priest' now; he might just as well have been a cardinal. He was to meet Adolphe Thiers, the President, several times that year.

16

BACK TO THE WILDS

'Look at these, Armand,' said Father Jamet as he handed David a pile of newspaper cuttings. 'I saved these for you.' 'You're famous now,' he added as an afterthought.

That night, on the occasion of writing home, David wrote:

> Since my return to China the newspapers at Shanghai, the Evening Courier, the Shanghai Budget, and the French Shanghai Nouvelliste, have reproduced portions of the European publications of my diaries and given me a reputation which tires me. However, these are things I cannot prevent and which may have their good side, though they are not to my taste.

David had returned to China in March 1872, after a brief period of recuperation in Europe. Before returning to Peking he set off from Shanghai on a brief exploration of the Chekiang province. Despite the many pirates who infested the East China Sea, David made the crossing of the Bay of Hangchow to Ningpo in a small junk. From Ningpo he travelled as far as Kiu-tcheu and then turned back so as not to miss his passage from Shanghai back to Peking.

The third and longest expedition David had in mind was to explore the hitherto little-known interior region of the Chin Ling mountains in the provinces of Shensi and Shansi.

Taking two young Chinese converts to act as hunters David set off from Peking on his mammoth journey to the unknown heart of central China, a journey which would take him over two years to accomplish. It was 2 October 1872. Little did David know that he had taken his last farewell of the capital. They headed first for Paoting in Honan province.

From Honan they journeyed on to Singan, the capital of Shensi province, and from Singan made several expeditions into the Chin Ling mountains and surrounding regions, collecting everything they could of interest and novelty

A view over the formidable maze of loess-clefts that occur in Shansi province.

in the way of plants and animals. David climbed several mountains well over 5,000 ft (1,525 m) which were of special interest, being very rich in deposits of coal. It was now mid-January 1873. He journeyed south to Mienhsien, in the valley of Hanching, along which the Han river flowed on its way to link up with the great Yangtze river at Hankow. On reaching the Han David, who had been travelling mostly on foot for several months, decided to go by river to Hankow.

This time the intrepid explorer was forced to undergo even more perils and hardships than on his second journey of exploration to Szechwan, and this time he was not merely a bystander at the wreckage brought to boats and lives by the dangerous rapids: he was actually shipwrecked himself and though he escaped with his life, he lost all his baggage and a large part of his valuable collection of natural history specimens. Finally, after much privation and with literally only the clothes he had on, he was able to reach Kiukiang and then Nantchang, capital of the province of Kiangsi. It was the bad season and there was much disease in the province: he contracted the high fever which had already laid low his two Chinese companions. Despite their illness the three continued their march to the village of Kientchang. Fortunately, a mission house and college was situated at Tsitou, three leagues from Kientchang. On reaching the mission David had reached the point of collapse; indeed he was almost dead.

He spent the whole of summer, 1873, completely bedridden because of his illness. It was not until October of that year that there was any improvement in his condition.

No sooner did he feel a little better than he very unwisely set off exploring the chain of mountains that separated Kiangsi province from the province of Fukien. It turned out to be an agonising trip; his two faithful Chinese companions were reduced to crying from fatigue and exhaustion. It took them six hours to ford one river, using ropes tied round their waists for fear of being carried away by the swift currents. By the time they reached the village of Koaten David was in agony with chronic bronchial ague, and he was

182

so critically ill that on 11 November he was given the last sacraments of the Church. It was patently obvious that he was too ill to continue any further scientific exploration. Not only had he developed inflammation of the lungs; moreover his two Chinese helpers were also seriously ill. They stayed on at the village for some weeks, in the hope of regaining some of their strength before beginning the arduous return to Tsitou. Finally, though still burning with fever and suffering from chronic bronchitis, David began the six days' march back to Tsitou. Every day the march necessitated negotiating steep mountains and scrambling down equally precipitous descents.

David was full of praise and admiration for the devotion, patience and forbearance of his two companions. Despite their illness and suffering, David recorded in his diary, 'they are quiet and never make a complaint or even a gesture of discontent'. By the time of his third journey David had spent much time living very closely with the Chinese – indeed, as one of them. His love of them had grown with his more intimate knowledge; he no longer spoke of them disparagingly as he sometimes did in his earlier journeys.

After six weeks in Tsitou David decided to return to Kiukiang: he was too ill to continue further exploration. Though burning with fever and shivering with ague, he set off in an open boat, clasping like gold the bamboo crates that held his precious natural history specimens. From Kiukiang he travelled on to Shanghai, which he reached on 5 April 1874. By now his health had broken down completely. This was not surprising since he had travelled a distance, often on foot, of over 3,000 miles (5,000 km), during which time he had collected enough in the way of important new natural history specimens to fill ten large crates. In the field of botany alone and after losses by various accidents, David had found, during his three expeditions, more than 1,570 plants, including over 250 *new* species and ten or eleven *new* genera.

David was sitting in a bamboo chair, in the garden of the Vincentian house, a straw hat keeping the glare out of his eyes. 'It's for you, Father,' the young Chinese boy said as he handed the tired, recuperating man a letter. David turned the envelope over; it was marked 'Bishop's Residence'. This was the letter David was waiting for. Slowly he opened it. It was from Monseigneur Desflèches. His great friend Monseigneur Baldus had passed on, to be succeeded by Monseigneur Desflèches.

'My Dear Armand', the letter began. 'Greetings . . .'

David's eyes ran down the page quickly to the paragraphs he knew would contain the news.

> I enclose the medical report from Dr Martin of the French Legation. I do not understand all the complicated medical

terminology. I discussed the matter with him a few days ago, and he advised you should be sent back to Europe to regain your health. His advice is that you should not be sent back to China again as your health could not take that. I explained to him that, apart from your faith, science was the most important consideration in your life, that the study of science, the exploration of the marvels of the hand of God, were the expression of your religion.

But Dr Martin was adamant. To stay any longer in this climate or to return to it again will kill you.

I have considered the matter with some of the Fathers.

It is with great reluctance that I must tell you that we are making arrangements for you to return to France at the earliest possible opportunity. I know how this will break your heart, but it is your health and life that drives us to this reluctant decision. I am sure you will understand.

With fraternal greetings,

Yours in Our Lord Jesus Christ

Richard †

Vicar Apostolic.

Slowly David rose out of his chair. Using his favourite butterfly net as a stick he hobbled into his room. This was the news he had feared most. The tears welled in his eyes. All those plans for further explorations – and there were so many scientific riches in this marvellous country – all would now go by the board. He had set his heart on seeing Lake Koko Nor before he left the Celestial Empire. The lake, over 1,500 square miles (2,400 square km) in extent and at an altitude over 10,000 feet (3,050 m), had always fascinated him. There were so many legends about it: that it had once been a fertile valley but was then flooded by a demon by means of an underground tunnel from Lhasa, and many more. And he had been so near to it!

He picked up the crucifix that his parents had given him at his ordination which stood on his rickety table, and wiped his eyes so that he could read the piece of paper which he kept under it. Tightening his grip round the crucifix he read the words from the Song of Solomon:

The end of the road for David; his health had
broken down completely. He had travelled
more than 3,000 miles (5,000 km) through
great hardships, and often on foot. 'You must
return to France – this time for good.'

This is my Beloved and my Friend; He is altogether desirable. If
such a Being commands me, I will gladly obey, because without Him, once He has been seen, everything is empty and vain.

On 3 January 1874 David bade farewell for the last time to the country he loved
so much as he watched the skyline of Shanghai disappear beyond the horizon.

185

POSTSCRIPT

Did David send any live giant pandas to Europe? Helen Fox, in her introduction to *Abbé David's Diary* writes:

> Among the animals discovered by Abbé David the giant panda, *Ailuropoda melanoleucus*, created the greatest interest. It can be imagined what a stir was caused when the panda arrived at the Jardin d'Acclimation. For a while it was the only example in Europe, but the first to come did not long survive its transference from the mountains of Szechwan.

Could this have been the adult female giant panda that the hunters brought to David on 1 April 1869? In his diary David does not say whether the animal was alive or dead. In 1951 Jessie Dobson, Curator of the Hunterian Museum at the Royal College of Surgeons in London, stated in the Proceedings of the Zoological Society of London (No. 121) that Père David had brought live giant pandas for the Paris Zoo.

> For convenience of transport the young giant panda brought to David on March 23, 1869, had been killed by the local hunters, but later several others were obtained alive and sent to Paris. (In 1888 the Jardin des Plantes had four Giant Pandas, the only examples outside China.)

Unfortunately Miss Dobson had mislaid her notes, which contained a great deal of information from original sources. But she was adamant that her claim was based on very sound evidence. In a paper given by David himself in 1888 on *La Faune Chinoise* he stated that only four museum examples of *Ailuropoda* existed at that time and all of these he had brought back from Muping. Unfortunately, he does not state whether the examples are living or not.

Some people argue that Helen Fox was confused between the giant panda and the lesser panda, which was also introduced to Europe in 1869. But in her statement there is no confusion: she is referring quite specifically to *Ailuropoda melanoleucus*, the giant panda. And there was certainly no confusion between the two animals in David's mind: to him the giant panda was a bear – *Ursus melanoleucus* – and the lesser panda was a *chan-che-cua*.

Others argue that a giant panda could not have survived the harsh conditions of transportation over such a long distance a century ago. But Père David's deer, equally rare, and many other animals, survived, so why not the giant panda? Perhaps the question will remain a mystery, just as the existence of the giant panda itself remained a mystery for centuries.

BIBLIOGRAPHY

PRIMARY SOURCES (Armand David)

Journal d'un voyage en Mongolie fait en 1866, published in the Bulletin appended to *Nouvelles Archives du Muséum d'Histoire Naturelle de Paris*, Vols III and IV, Paris, 1867, 1868.

Journal d'un Voyage dans le centre de la Chine et dans le Thibet Oriental, published in the Bulletin appended to *Nouvelles Archives du Muséum d'Histoire Naturelle de Paris*, Vols VII, IX, X, Paris, 1872, 1873, 1874.

Journal de mon troisième voyage d'exploration dan L'Empire Chinois, Libraire Hachette et Cie, Paris, 1875.

David (Armand) and Oustalet, M. E., *Les Oiseaux de la Chine*, 2 vols, Paris, 1877.

Franchet, M. A., *Nouvelles Archives du Muséum d'Histoire Naturelle*, series 2, Vols 5, 6, 7, *Plantae Davidianae ex Sinarum Imperio. Plantes de la Mongolie Chinoise et de la Chine Septentrionale et Centrale*; Vols 8, 10, *Plantes du Thibet Oriental (Province de Moupine) 1883–1888*.

Milne-Edwardes H. and A., *Recherches pour servir a l'Histoire Naturelle des Mammifères*, G. Masson, Libraire de L'Académie de Médicine, Paris, 1868–1874.

Milne-Edwardes, A., *Nouvelles Archives du Muséum d'Histoire Naturelle*, Vol. II, Paris, 1866.

Oberthuer, C., *Etudes d'Entomologie*, Paris, 1876.

Abbé David's Diary, translated Fox, Helen M., Harvard University Press, 1949.

SECONDARY SOURCES

Chawarth-Masters, J. L., 'The discoverer of the giant panda', in *Zoo Life, Journal of the Zoological Society of London*, 1946.

Darnatz, J. B., 'Un grand naturaliste basque. A. David', *Bulletin de Société des Sciences, Lettres et Etudes*, 1929.

Fournier, P., 'Voyages et découvertes scientifiques des missionaires naturalistes français', *Encyclopédie Biologique*, X, Paul Lechevalier et fils, Paris, 1932.

Hance, H. F. 'Notes on some plants from China', *Linnaean Society Journal*, XIII, London, 1871.

Huc, E. R. and J. Gabet, *Travels in Tartary, Thibet and China*, 1844–6, translated Wm. Hazlitt, Geo. Routledge and Sons Ltd., London, 1928.

Morris, R. and D., *Men and Pandas*, Hutchinson, London, 1966.

Perry, R. *The World of the Giant Panda*, Cassell, London, 1969.

Proceedings of Zoological Society of London, No. 121, 1951.

ACKNOWLEDGEMENTS

BLACK AND WHITE ILLUSTRATIONS

British Library

Barba, Gustav (ed.), *La Chine*, Paris, 1858: p. 139.

Bazin de Malpière, *La Chine*, 1825–39: pp. 28, 29, 140, 148.

Bishop, Mrs I. L., *Chinese Pictures*, Cassell & Co., London, 1900: pp. 20, 30, 34, 42, 53, 93, 98, 124, 145, 154.

Bishop, Mrs I. L., *The Yangtze Valley and Beyond*, John Murray, London, 1899: Frontispiece, pp. 36, 52, 94, 127, 141, 146, 147, 149, 164.

Darnatz, J. B., 'Un Grand Naturaliste Basque. A David', *Bulletin de Société de Sciences, Lettres et Etudes*, Paris, 1929: p. 8.

Dukes, E. J., *Along River and Road in Fukien*, 1886: p. 129.

Fortune, R., *A Residence Among the Chinese*, John Murray, London, 1857: p. 99.

Fortune, R., *Three Years Wanderings in the Northern Provinces of China*, John Murray, London, 1847: p. 104.

Fournier, P., 'Voyages et découvertes scientifiques des missionaires naturalistes francais', *Encyclopédie Biologique*, X, Paul Lechevalier et fils, Paris, 1932. p. 185.

Huc, E., *Souvenirs d'un Voyage dans la Tartaire et le Tibet 1844–66*, Vols I and II, J. M. Planchet, The Lazarist Mission, Peking, 1924: pp. 23, 38, 48, 58, 83, 84.

Huc, E., *Travels in Tartary, Tibet and China during 1844–66*, Vols I and II, London office of National Illustrated Library, London, 1852: pp. 86, 87, 88, 89.

Huc, E. (trans. W. Hazlitt), *Travels in Tartary*, A. Knopf, New York, 1927: pp. 32, 59.

Moges, Marquis de, *Recollections of Baron Gros's Embassy to China and Japan in 1857/8*, Richard Griffin & Co., London, 1860: pp. 101, 105.

Pratt, A. E., *To the Snows of Tibet Through China*, Longman, Green & Co., London, 1892: pp. 131, 138.

Reid, W. J., *Through Unexplored Asia*, Dana Estes & Co., Boston, 1899: pp. 44, 47.

Rockhill, W. W., *The Land of the Lamas*, Longman, Green & Co., London, 1891: pp. 45, 160.

Sadler, Rev. J., *True Celestials*, S. W. Partridge & Co., London, 1891: pp. 127, 133.

Swinhoe, R., *Narrative of the North China Campaign of 1860*, Smith, Elder & Co. Cornhill, London, 1861: p. 68.

Thomson, John, *Through China With a Camera*, A. Constable & Co., Washington, 1898: pp. 31, 60, 103, 122.

Wells-Williams, S., *The Middle Kingdom*, Vol I, Charles Scribner's Sons, New York, 1883: pp. 22, 130, 182.

Wright, G. N., China, *Its Scenery, Architecture, Social Habits, etc.*, Vols I–IV, Fisher Son & Co., London, 1843: pp. 25, 30, 43, 55, 76, 97, 107, 113, 144, 151.

Yule, Sir Henry, *The Book of Ser Marco Polo*, Vol II, John Murray, London, 1903: pp. 155, 162, 169.

Zoological Society of London: pp. 15, 33, 85, 166, 167, 174.

Zoo Life, No. 3, 1946: Back Cover.

COLOUR PLATES

British Library

Franchet, M. A., *Nouvelles Archives du Muséum d'Histoire Naturelle*, Series 2, Vol 8, Paris 1878: Plate 10.

Milne-Edwardes, A; *Nouvelles Archives du Muséum d'Histoire Naturelle*, Vol II, Paris, 1866: Plate 14.

Milne-Edwardes, H. and A., *Recherches pour servir a l'Histoire Naturelle des Mammifères*, Atlas 2, Paris, 1868–74: Plates 1, 2, 5, 6, 7, 8, 9, 11, 12, 13, 15, 18, 19.

Oberthuer C., *Etudes d'Entomologie*, Paris, 1876–1902: Plate 4.

Zoological Society of London

David, A. and Oustalet, M., *Les Oiseaux de la Chine*, Vol II, Paris, 1877: Plates 3, 16, 17, 20.

INDEX

Page numbers in italic refer to black-and-white illustrations; colour plates fall between pages 64 and 65.